AF619320

DEAR GOD,

Letters to God

Editor: Kathleen Becker Blease

Copy Editor and Proofreader: Frank W. Kresen

Cover Design: Evan Sorosky

Interior Design/Publishing: Kim Walsh

First Printing 2021

ISBN Number: 9798985014204

kenstearns.com

Table of Contents

Acknowledgments

Writing *Dear God* has been an amazing journey, one which would not have been possible without the love and support of family, friends, and so many other people. I will never forget the encouragement from my daughters, Alexandria and Danielle, over the years of this project, to share my life experiences, and their never-ending support for all things Dad. Love you two.

Thank you, Harrienath Pillay, for telling me I should write a book and for giving me so many of the ideas that I am pursuing today in such a short and powerful sidelines chat. Never underestimate the power of believing in someone else.

Special thanks to Alonso Pasion, who inspired me to take these dusty old letters out of the drawer and begin to write again. I'm forever grateful, my friend.

A special thank-you to my brothers for their feedback, guidance, challenges, and, finally, endless support. (Also for kicking my ass every day growing up and teaching me what it is to be tough.) I get a lot of my *never give up* attitude from their lessons.

Finally, a big thanks to the professionals around me who made sure my ideas were expressed powerfully, readably, and articulately. Evan Sorosky, Cover Art. Kathleen Becker Blease, developmental editor. Frank Kresen, copy editor and proofreader. Kimberly Walsh, all things design and publishing.

About the Book

Sometime in my early fifties, I started writing while traveling instead of my usual reading. Over the past 20 years, I had spent a lot of time in airports and planes while living in Asia and working in 15 countries, and something had changed inside of me. I was no longer a consumer of content. I became its producer. It was inside me and needed to get out.

Around this time, my mother was aging quickly past 90, and, as she did, her faith became a bigger and bigger piece of her life, comforting her deeply during her last years, then days, then hours. The closer she got to death, the more her faith's depth and conviction seemed to double down.

My mother's faith: The depth of it truly impressed me. It also confused me and awed me. She never seemed to waver in her belief that God truly watched over her, her children, her life. She prayed without hesitation, with dedication. And she prayed as she was passing away. I hope that one day I can have the same conviction in life that she had in her faith.

I was raised Catholic and was an altar boy. Then, like many other young people, I drifted away from the Church and religion in general. Over the years that I've lived and worked in Asia, I've been exposed to many other religions, cultures, and belief systems; their different ways of looking at life impacted me. I suddenly believed in everything and nothing at the same time.

My own faith, my own spirituality, was something I hadn't confronted. I hadn't faced who I was and what I believed or didn't believe after all these years.

One day, on a plane headed back to Asia from a visit to see my mother, I was feeling a little sad. I took out my notes folder, ripped out a blank page, printed on it the word "Faith," and started writing. And that became the first letter in *Dear God.* What had started as a few letters became an idea and then a project to somehow better understand my own spirituality, what I've learned over the years, and what remains unresolved.

I wanted to share these letters and my own journey to inspire you to reflect on who you are and what kind of legacy you want to leave. What do you believe? What don't you believe? What kind of impact will you have left behind when you are gone? I know that there are many people who are on a similar journey and can connect with the messages in my conversations with God. My hope is to share them with as many people as possible.

About the Author

Ken Stearns is a grandfather, father, midwestern boy, writer, speaker, photographer, and lyricist.

His writings reflect his last-child position, with a father who passed away just as Ken was starting his own family and learning to become a father himself. Those father-son moments that were missed over the last 30 years of his own family struggles were side by side with his career success. Additionally, his mother living into her early 90s and displaying a deep conviction of faith led him to question his own faith, spirituality, and relationship with God.

In this, his first book, *Dear God*, Ken tries to make sense in his own way about how all his experiences and upbringing have led him to look at life — not in a religious way but in a practical way. His collection of 48 conversations with God looks at how to live and work with ourselves first, with those closest to us, with others, and, finally, with God.

Growing up in a Chicago suburb, in a perfect American midwestern 1970s dream life, Ken was gifted a unique view of Americana, before he challenged his comfort zone by moving to South Carolina for university, where he called Columbia home for three years before graduating. He soon moved to California, where, for the next 15 years, he started a family and began his professional insurance career. He then moved to Asia to live and work for the next 20 years.

As he winds down his corporate career, the influence of his travels, experiences, exposure to cultures, religions, and music is beginning to emerge. Ken continues to write, with several projects in the works, and he enjoys photography and writes music. Look for these projects as time goes on.

I. Book of Self

Letters to God

Dear God

Books of Prayer

I. Book of Self

by Ken Stearns

Yesterday

Today

Tomorrow

Yesterdays

Letting go of the past

Dear God,

Memories are a funny thing. I have such a seemingly eclectic collection of memories going back to probably the age of four or five, many happy memories and a few I'd rather forget. There are some I should remember better. Others I remember in vivid detail, and they even evoke the emotions of that moment, a hearty laugh, a painful tear. These memories—part of my story, part of who I have become—are embedded into the fabric of my soul and ride along with me on the journey of life.

There is so much good in there, so many fun times, proud moments, experiences I would never change. And as I carry those with me, they are an inspiration and a joy, an energizer, a confidence builder.

But there are also memories of so many things I *wished* I had done. Missed birthdays and chances to say a kind word when it mattered most. Promises made, then broken. Disappointments I've caused, a harsh word, a short temper. And the people I've let down. My loved ones, family, friends, myself. The pain I have caused others and my disappointment in myself. These are the memories I should forget. The ones I don't want to relive. The pain is still real, the emotions unstable, and these memories take me where I don't want to go.

In my darkest times, the battle of my yesterdays rages in my head. The good memories fade, and the ones I wish I could forget take center stage. They play to a full house of anxiety and fear, regret, pity, anger, and hate. It's a play that runs every night, over and over again in my head as I lie down to sleep.

Can I find a way to let go of the bad memories, the negative emotions of the past? Can I unburden myself of these thoughts and free my mind, my heart, and soul? Can I learn to let go of yesterday and package all these bad memories in a jar and bury them or burn them out of my mind so I can let go of the past that gives me pain?

What if I were to truly let go? What if I were to decide that all my yesterdays were just that—in my past? They are memories. They cannot touch me today or tomorrow, and they're not something I need to keep. Sure, memories are there. They are part of me, part of who I am, and even the bad ones have some good, such as a lesson learned that I should not forget.

But I'm changing how my yesterdays hold me down. How they keep me bound in the past, not living in today, and certainly not envisioning tomorrow. I can let go of the past, free myself from those chains. What a feeling, what a weight off my shoulders. Waking up with only thoughts of today, and when today is done, tomorrow will come. I am excited, cannot sleep thinking of what's possible.

The weight of the memories, the pain, the hurts, matter no more. Now that I have freed myself from my yesterdays, I can reconcile with them and regain control. My past becomes useful, richer, deeper, making me more resilient. All that's left of my yesterdays are the lessons and a freedom from the pain, a freedom that lifts me up and propels me forward to tomorrow, more determined, more powerful, more alive.

Dear God, help me let go of the past, my yesterdays, the burdens that weigh me down and cloud my mind. Even though the battle

rages every night between my heart and my mind and my soul, with my prayers to you, what seemed big becomes small, and what seemed insurmountable is merely a task to do.

Yesterday

Unburdened

Dear God,

In school as a young boy, I had a chance to be an altar boy. Since my mom was a devout Catholic, I volunteered. It was probably the first time I knowingly did something for someone else to make them happy, to show them I cared. I have been to many 6:00 a.m. masses during the week, when only the most faithful came on those Chicago winter mornings. Waking up was next to impossible. The cold room, the frozen car driving through snowy dark streets.

During those four years, I served at Christmas services with the entire parish there—generations of families dressed for the annual celebration. I served at funerals, where people came to bless the deceased, remember them fondly, and celebrate their lives. I watched as joyous young parents baptized their babies, cleansing their souls, and I helped with weddings, where two people became as one in your eyes.

Every "event" in church is a celebration. A celebration of life. From giving thanks and being grateful, to celebrating life coming, life going, and two becoming one. I have learned over my life that this happens in the Church, in the Temple, and in the Mosque. All houses of worship accept our burdens and share our joys.

No one leaves your houses of worship with a heavy heart. No one carries their burdens home. We feel the weight of our yesterdays lifted. We smile to each other. No. We smile *into* each other. Our souls touch for a moment with pure happiness, pure content. For that moment, we understand and share what being unburdened from our yesterdays feels like.

If I could measure the weight of my yesterdays and truly understand how much I carry around with me, could I appreciate the physical toll, the spiritual toll it takes on me and those around me? Pushing myself forward each day, living today, driving myself through the day, but being weighed down by my yesterdays. What's the real extra cost to my mind, my heart, and soul?

How can I understand that, measure that?

If I could quantify the energy it takes, I could learn to let go, drop the baggage of the past, feel the weightlessness of living in today, and accomplish so much. Feel so free, so happy, so content. I could imagine the feeling of truly letting go and the ease with which I can tackle new things, manage my life daily without the constant weight of the baggage I carry.

Dear God, please give me the joy of waking in the morning and looking myself in the mirror eye to eye, seeing—no, **feeling*****—the weightlessness of self-love.***

Yesterday

Finding the good

Dear God,

As I get older, it's interesting to watch as some people, no matter the situation, find the good things in the journey. They seem to bounce through life in a protective bubble and always land on their feet. It's not because they have no difficulties. It's that somehow, no matter what happens, they find the good part of it. And that's what becomes their story. Not the loss. Not the injury and the hurt. Not the pain.

It's not that they are lucky in life. Their difficulties are just not what define their day or week, month, year, life. But they become part of their fabric. They're woven into their experience, making them deeper, more resilient, more concentrated and focused on what's important in life, whisking past life's nuisances with vigor, swatting the bad memories and pain away, and snatching the lessons and fun stories along the way.

They collect the valuable memories and lessons, the experiences from life. And they arm themselves with them. They are no longer baggage to be carried around like an altar to their hurts and regrets, but a strong armor, a thick skin with which to confidently attack life, knowing that no matter the outcome, they collect something valuable and move on.

My mother was one of these people. Even as she aged, she was a positive person. She always had the positive part of every story that made up her 93 years, even the tragic ones. While the pain was there—and we knew what parts of life she prayed on—her stories always revolved around how the outcome led to something positive. She knew how to find the good in the events along the way through her life.

Her third child, my sister Nancy, had Down syndrome. Ultimately, she was institutionalized with the state. It weighed on my mom heavily, and, I am sure, in her prayers to you, God, she asked for forgiveness for not being able to care for Nancy and for sending her to a hospital. She said it was the hardest thing to do, but she knew it was the best thing, and I always felt like she had found the good in what was a beyond-painful decision.

She knew instinctively how to let go of the past and value the good from it, and to leverage that. She knew how to live in the day while somehow manifesting through all of this a happy life. Maybe it's her character that I find in these types of people, and over time I naturally gravitate to them.

Dear God, help me to find the good in all things bad, all bad outcomes, all bad situations. Give me a hopeful heart and a strong character to survive life's challenges and to be grateful for what I have. Help me to take with me in life an unburdened past and an appreciation for the good along the way.

Yesterday

Moving forward

Dear God,

Aren't all the religions that reach up to you following the same path? Don't they all focus on us conquering ourselves first? Our own thoughts and actions, the self. And once we are right with ourselves, only then can we be right with the people close to us—and *all* people. Only then can we hope to be right with you.

If we can conquer ourselves first—learn to let go of the past, measure the impact of letting go by understanding the energy it creates, the forward energy, the momentum, the powerful impact as we truly let go—then that weight is lifted. The energy that's needed to drag around with us the weight of those negative thoughts is huge. Releasing that weight and not having to pull it gives us an incredible new power to move ahead in life at full energy and focus.

Christianity has confession, Judaism *viddui*, and Islam *tawbah*. Buddhism has its confessional, too. All your followers are seeking forgiveness through self-reflection and acceptance and cleansing.

Moving forward is all about leveraging the release and its value for lifting this off our shoulders, both one time and for a lifetime, removing the drag it creates as we journey through life.

Our negative self-talk, regrets about yesterdays, and repeating what happened and what didn't happen. How that hurts us. Continues to hurt us. All that negativity has a weight, has an emotional gravitational value, and it truly is holding us back.

Once I let it go, once I decide it is past and behind me and has zero impact on my tomorrows, there is a huge release of energy with the weight of this gone. There's a momentum created, and less work is required to move ahead daily at the same pace.

I can imagine freedom from my yesterdays, freeing my soul, my mind, my heart and moving effortlessly through life, empowered by letting go of the past and focusing on the outcomes of today.

If I were to spend less time thinking about yesterday and embrace the ease with which I can live in today and the momentum I can carry into tomorrow, what is not possible? Nothing can hold me back or take away my future, except my own mind.

Dear God, help me accept and let go of my yesterdays; let me live in and be grateful for today while planning my tomorrows. Give me the strength and courage to face yesterday, extract the good lessons, and use those in my life to serve you and others.

Yesterdays

As I wake today,
Please wash away
My sins, my past,
My yesterdays.

When I look in the mirror
Eye to eye
With the man I have become,
Can I weigh,
Can I measure,
Can I find the man
I can forgive?
'Cause at the end of the day,
I face the night
Needing peace of heart and mind.

The older I get,
The heavier the load,
Fearful at times.

Am I man enough to carry the load
Down the road,
Taking me home to you?

When I sleep tonight,
I'll wash away
My sins,
My past,
My yesterdays.

When I look in the mirror,
Eye to eye,
In love with the man I am,
I can weigh,
I can measure,
I can find the man
I can forgive.
'Cause at the end of the day,
I'll face the night

Having peace of heart and mind.

Today

Sunrise

Dear God,

What's more magnificent than the sunrise? Even the beauty of a thousand sunsets cannot match the vision of hope, life, birth—the rebirth that wraps itself in the sunrise.

In the darkness of night, God, I often find myself lost in the never-ending loop of replaying my day, focusing on the mistakes I made. The hard words, short temper. Missed chances to show compassion and empathy. Where I wasn't the best version of myself. Tossing and turning, waiting for the sunrise to ease my pain, settle my mind, restore the hope and grace with a new day.

When I travel, you've often seen me awake before your sunrise, there at the beach, or on my balcony, or sitting at breakfast alone. I am there waiting for the majesty of your creation. Alone in thought, reflecting, thinking of the day, of life.

Even before its arrival, the sunrise shows its soft hues on the night sky, forcing the moon aside. Roosters announce its arrival, birds sing its praise. Light is restored, hope is renewed, and we all awake summoned by its power. Watching the colors change, the palette of your choosing for that moment—the blues, orange, purples and everything in-between-—float across the sky, crawl across the land as the sun rises on the horizon, casting its warm life-giving rays across the land.

I feel as if anything is possible in the morning light. Today becomes a vehicle to achieve our dreams, to be the best version of ourselves that we can be. I feel like I can harvest the power of the morning and everything it represents. Capture it, use it, share it. The fountain of hope, the endless possibilities for tomorrow that I hold in my hands with this new day.

The idea that everything I do and say, everything I act on, has a multiplying effect and can last 100,000 tomorrows excites me, scares me, ultimately inspires me to make the most of the opportunity. I can sleep at the end of today knowing that I did what I had planned to do, then wake up tomorrow ready again.

Morning is broken, and yesterday has now faded into the glory of today. I can feel hope being replenished in my own soul, my doubts lifted, my energies focused on the day. This day. My yesterdays only bring a smile, and tomorrows, while there on my horizon, are not the focus. It is today that is in view. Its fragility and its virility. The day is fragile yet life-giving, so we must take care to seize the opportunities we have.

Dear God, never take away the magic of the sunrise. Never let me miss one, miss the chance to marvel at its majesty and wonder what the day holds for each of us. Never let me miss what hope you give with the light that touches the darkest corners of life, the darkest corners of the mind. Let my childlike wonderment of this creation amaze me and inspire me each time.

Today

Enjoy this moment

Dear God,

How often do you watch people go from one rushed moment to another? They live their whole lives in concentric circles of tasks, going from one day to the next in a frantic cycle that never seems to end. I know how easily that happens for me, how little I stop and reflect during the day.

As the dawn turns into day, there's the danger of being swept away with a list of things to do, the things we haven't done, where we fell short yesterday, and the thoughts of what will happen tomorrow.

Before I allow myself to rush into the day, it's important to be thankful, grateful for what I have in life and the moment I am in. No matter how small, no matter my situation, there is always something for which I can give thanks.

Why can't I find the time to truly enjoy the perfection of your creation and my own place here in the synchronicity of trillions of galaxies? Spinning, rotating, elliptical, dancing universes dependent on one another for millennia, until the ever-expanding dimensions collide, compact, explode, only to dance again millennia on millennia, galaxy on galaxy.

Even though I know this and appreciate it, I don't sit back, relax, and ponder my place in all of your grand intelligent design often enough. I am grateful to be alive in this time and living this way, grateful for what's been afforded to me and what I've earned. But I'm not grateful in a way that is regular and thoughtful.

During my working life, the way to motivate and inspire people to work with difficult challenges has been to reward them. Over time, money became less important, and it was the recognition and gratitude for their efforts that memorialized the months and years of their hard work and the impact they had on others. We thanked them. We praised their work.

The best leaders I've worked with had two powerful qualities. They were grateful and personal. They knew how to show gratitude to their team members when they hit goals or finished projects. Even more, they knew how to make the moment personal and special, creating a memory. It was the power of making gratitude personal and memorializing the moment. People wanted to be around that, and individuals and teams would do what it took to be a part of it.

I want to find gratitude. I want to embrace it, think about it, and share it. I want to be present in the now. This day, in everything I do, I want to value the people I meet, strangers and friends, family and co-workers. Gratitude is a very positive energy, and it transfers to others very easily. It helps us to take on the day with a positive attitude and to get through tough situations. I want to be grateful and to make each moment a destination and to memorialize it.

Dear God, keep putting those moments in front of me, the ones that make me stop in amazement. Remind me to find the little ones, even when I am down. You know I appreciate them. Give me those triggers to pause—I need them, really—to take a moment, that snapshot, that destination, and recognize how special life is.

Today

Value of today

Dear God,

What about today? Today feels like nothing. Between thousands of yesterdays and thousands of tomorrows, what needs to happen today or should have happened yesterday that can't wait for tomorrow? Today feels like a snapshot in time, just a single frame in an endless movie that is the sum of my history.

But I know there is more. Intuitively, I know there is more. What if each day mattered, if each day between my yesterdays and tomorrows felt heavy and hard, felt full? Would I wake before the sun and connect the great things I see? The construction of millions of yesterdays and the infinite tomorrows. And rejoice in the moment of the everlasting tomorrows. Plan my day, my actions and deeds, my words, to make the Earth spin a little faster and the sun shine a little brighter for me, my family, my loved ones, just a little bit.

Certainly, such an important day requires thought, some planning and effort. It's worthy of something more than just waking and wondering what to do today. Today links all my yesterdays to all my tomorrows. Like a chain that never ends, from father to son, mother to daughter, each link carrying the weight of a thousand generations, a thousand galaxies, the heaviest cross gifted with the strength of Hercules. But must I use yesterday to plan today, and use today to plan tomorrow, like a DNA strand that contains thousands of years of my history?

Even the smallest accomplishment of the day has a lasting impact on our life. That's why it's so important to focus on the most important thing on my list today, that one thing I will do for myself, my family and friends, and my work that will have the most impact. That's where the most value lies.

With thousands of tomorrows ahead of us, it's the small effort of what I do today, compared to the expectations of the long term, that articulates why I should never waste a day. Put first the most impactful goal, the one with the largest potential impact to my life and to the lives of others. Execute it with all my might.

While I write this and discover this secret, I weep at the time I have wasted. So many todays wasted. But even one more today feels so powerful. The enormous power that resides in just one today brightens my soul, makes my pen so light, the ink so fluid. Yet at the same time, the responsibility makes it heavy. How weak is each link in my chain of life, and how heavy the task to harden my days ahead, to forge them into a steel that carries the load of a thousand tomorrows, pull me up, tie down my loads, hold the dreams of my children, safely anchor my faith in myself.

Dear God, from this today, and all my todays, I promise to you and to myself that I'll make each one count, live in that today like I have no tomorrows. Live like each day is the last. Guide me to make the most of each day here on this Earth, so few and so precious each day is. However short my time, the impact of my life can last generations, so forgive me for the many days I have wasted.

Today

Sunset

Dear God,

The sunset in all its majesty announces the end of today, welcomes the night sky and the glory of the heavens in the deep of night. The beauty of a sunset, no matter where I am, God, always amazes me. The bright orange sun, the blue skies fading as the sun kisses the edge of the Earth, the deep colors of orange, purple, and blue emerging and melting across the sky, twirling, swirling, as though you're playing with finger paints. Each night gently fades to gray and to black as the twinkle of distant stars appears, then our own sister planets. Never the same, always perfect. Thank you.

Now, time to enjoy the wonderment of the heavens, to gaze upon and understand and appreciate the millions of yesterdays dancing in delight with the millions of tomorrows yet to come. Just further proof of the value of today. The power of today, with its impact that we create, vibrates into the universe as positive waves, lasting millennia.

As the sun surrenders to tomorrow and signifies the end of the day, it's time to cure my work, my thoughts, my deeds. Just as I began the day in gratitude, now I end with reflection and take an inventory. To relive the day, what happened versus the plan, and the emotions, the feelings, the actions. There's always something to learn. And when I do it often and without judgment, it's such a powerful tool.

With my reflection in hand, it's time to think how it affects or influences my plans for tomorrow. What I think about and write down, plan for, share and revisit becomes my tomorrows. Before I finish the day in bed, it's a great time to write down my affirmations, challenges and opportunities, goals and to-do's. Let them cure overnight. Let the power of my mind guide me.

This daily effort, its focus and repetition, the almost-mantric approach that focuses on what's important in my life, this specific goal leads to a manifestation. It's living, breathing, doing everything in a today mode to build a sustainable tomorrow. I imagine a kinetic energy from the focused long-term view, the continuous effort ultimately creating its own vibration, its own energy, becoming self-sustaining, becoming kinetic.

Finally, like so much of nature, it's in all my DNA. Time to gather those closest to me. Those I depend on, those who depend on me, family and loved ones. Those with whom I close each today and welcome tomorrows, and with whom I built thousands of yesterdays. Rest my body. Rest my mind and spirit.

Dear God, show me the majesty of the sunset each night so I can pause and be reminded to share my gratitude with you and others. About small things, big things, anything. Let the close of the day remind me to settle all things outstanding, review my plans for tomorrow, and get a good rest.

Tomorrow

One place where yesterdays don’t matter

Dear God,

When I lie in bed at night and close my eyes, I take an inventory of the day, the week, and at times, my life. Working through my yesterdays, I may ask forgiveness for things I've done or a word I've said. As my thoughts turn to tomorrow, next week, next year, I want to leave behind the small things and minimize the big ones. What's left of those big problems, those worries, those challenges when I need guidance and I talk with you? Asking for your help gives me all the courage I need. I know it's up to me, but having you there by my side gives me comfort and strength.

Even with you there, tomorrow is an unknown quantity, and it's easy to let my worry take control. Yesterdays are known, contained. But how do I manage the fear of what tomorrow may bring? There are so many things I cannot control, and the possibilities of what could go wrong are endless.

When I was in university, maybe my second year, I had a particularly tough year, with too many things to manage and worry about.

Finances while I was far away from home were tight and tricky. My dad's health was bad, and my classes were challenging. I had a job, a girlfriend, a social life. I was doing too much, and when I lay in bed and drifted off, I invariably had bad dreams, often waking up with searingly painful cramps in my calves. I was dreaming of all the things that I was sure were going to go wrong. Things that, of course, never happened.

Yet, every morning I would wake up and start the day anew, regardless of my yesterdays, no matter the situation—it was a new day and a chance to make tomorrow mine.

Isn't tomorrow really a place where yesterdays don't matter? Every day as the dawn breaks. Isn't that a cleansing, a washing away of yesterday? Tomorrow is unique in itself. No matter the situation, when we wake tomorrow, we can start fresh and new. Only what happens is what matters, not the endless possibilities of what could go wrong. If I've stumbled or fallen, I can get back up and take a first step. And if I am at the top, it's a chance to be grateful and find a way to keep rising.

Sure, my yesterdays matter. They determine where I start the day. And they matter as I harvest the sum of my yesterdays. But worrying about what that harvest brings is useless and counterproductive, harmful. It is what it is. Worrying won't change it. I'm letting that go, embracing the moment of today in my tomorrows.

Dear God, give me the courage to face the night, the possibility and wonder of tomorrow, the endless possibilities and opportunities, with strength, hope, and faith. Remove the doubt, the despair, and the worry. Let me sleep with the confidence and comforts under the safety of your watchful eye.

Tomorrow

Dreams, plans, actions become today

Dear God,

If tomorrow is a sum of my yesterdays, what's the sum of my tomorrows? Can I understand my future through my yesterdays? Am I bound to my future? Can I break these chains that are linked together, change the DNA, or am I bound to them like a slave unable to break free, destined to live out this life I have sown?

Can I change my path, through prayer, thoughts, and actions, and steer my tomorrows?

Shouldn't each day I awake bring hope that tomorrow is mine to hold in my hands, shaped by your love and my thoughts, my acts, my deeds?

My tomorrows are no longer bound by my yesterdays but a result of my todays. Day by day, step by step, my todays can have a positive impact on my tomorrows. Like the blacksmith that hammers away at the red-hot steel, shaping it to purpose. It matters not the shape he starts with as he uses fire, strength, and determination to control the outcome.

It does not matter at this point from where I start in life. The day-by-day approach, the compounding effect of days on days, weeks on weeks, gives me strength to carry on even when things are tough. Each small effort has a multiplying effect over time.

People who are the best in the world had planned to be the best in the world. They told the universe, set the course, and began the grueling work that was required to put them in the position to take the dreams into their arms.

It's their drive, their energy, their aura of certainty and invincibility that collect support along the way, a kinetic alignment, each effort fitting in, rounding out their efficiency, driving them toward completion. The universe, at one point, when it all fits together, pulls it forward to complete the puzzle, to balance the universe as it ever expands, fulfilling space and time.

The same is in my life. Positive energy, clear direction lead to others aligning, attraction, synergy, then manifesting outcomes.

Dear God, help me define my own destiny, announce it to the world, manifest it in my life and guide me to where I can be the best person I can be.

Tomorrow

Not a place, a destination, but a journey

Dear God,

You freed me from my yesterdays. Now I can leverage the powerful forces working on present value and future value by manifesting where I want to go. Doing what's important each day, my tomorrows become a way of life. Every tomorrow is in a way out of my control, but it's within the framework of what I have thought about, dreamt about, what I have internalized and done.

Why can't life be an endless cycle of reimagining the possible? Achieve one level, then go on to the next. Is that not what humanity has done for millennia? Why are we not focused, trained and educated, indoctrinated to dream like this? Shouldn't we manifest ourselves on where we want to go? Shouldn't we teach that? With humanity focused forward, collectively as a way of life, we can leverage the powerful forces that drive present and future values and sum them together as faster growth for everyone.

Kinetic energy is created by this alignment, with all forces vibrating in unison in the forward direction. Constantly focusing on todays in the most productive way. Manifesting desired states. Expressing gratitude and reflecting. If I drive life, if I'm proactive in thoughts and actions, the kinetic energy I can create is powerful.

Embedding this cycle of working my todays in the most productive way, manifesting my desired state, not focusing on mistakes but focusing on gratitude and reflection and repeat. The positive changes in my life are not linear, but if I follow this, they are exponential. Is this not humanity's biggest gift? To dream the impossible and find that all things are possible? It's there in mankind. When we do set our sights, mankind is never denied.

Can I live with this hope that my tomorrows will be more than the sum of yesterdays, a sum of all my hopes? Minus my fears. Minus my failures. Minus all my thoughts that cloud my mind but more of a storm of dreams, a rainbow of hopes, where dreams come true, a vision of what can be, should be, will be.

Just thinking and pondering the immense power of imagination—with which mankind has been gifted. And that imagination, if set to focus on solving problems or achieving something that has never been achieved or being the best in a field, can set the course like a skilled navigator managing the tides, the winds, the currents to bring us safely to port.

Dear God, my yesterdays dwarf my tomorrows, my todays weigh heavy, and every tomorrow is a blessing. This is my time to live for myself, enjoy the years of learning, dreaming, building. Help me to manifest my desired state, to navigate my journey, to not focus on my mistakes but to focus on what can be imagined with gratitude and reflection.

Tomorrow

A harvest that never ends

Dear God,

I recognize that there has never been a better time to be alive than today. Humanity is truly at its highest levels. Each generation is more advanced, more civil and peaceful, more intelligent and educated, healthier and better off than the last. So much of where mankind is today is due to the perpetual planting and harvesting of plans and works of previous generations, improving year by year, generation by generation.

The generation who lived from the early 1900s through the 1980s watched as horses were replaced by automobiles, trains by airplanes, and watched with awe as man landed on the moon and traveled back and forth from space in a rocket. They saw the invention of the radio take over life in the 1920s and television in the 1960s, and the birth of the internet. Every leap was not actually a leap but the result of thousands of todays, which made thousands of yesterdays and amazing and endless tomorrows. What they were witnessing was one harvest leading to the next.

The same is true of myself. I understand that I'm a better version of my younger self, once I release myself from my yesterdays, focus on today, and manifest the best version of myself. Day by day invest in each day, living that person, efforts multiplied over thousands of tomorrows. Thousands of harvests. Replanting again and days layered upon days, years upon the years.

Alive in the moment and focused on the future, I am unburdened from my past. No longer do I wear like a beast the yoke of my yesterdays, resigned to my karma. Knowing that my sentence will no longer end with me fulfilling my place in the complex weave of the universe, in the end discarded into the ashes of life.

Taking control of my tomorrows today. Knowing that regardless of where I am, I am in control of this day forward. From there, from that moment, I can build my tomorrows day by day, building my future harvests. Small at first, then bigger and bigger. Harvest, replant, reinvest, rework. Control what I can and manage the rest. A life dedicated to future outcomes.

Dear God, as I harvest my yesterdays, will you comfort me tomorrow? Can I seek solace in your bosom, as my tomorrows grow inside my head? Demons, my worst thoughts, my worst fears, I pray they can be transformed to be like the sunrise on the water, the orange sky of a new day's hope in the east. Full of promise. And a place where your love for me is reflected in my love for family, friends, and strangers.

Tomorrows

Tomorrows are my hope
Where I'll cast away my fears.
Time to gather up what I hold so dear.

Realize my dreams
That I've kept through all these years.
In a fall of my life,
Still fearful of these things.

Will the sum of yesterdays
Keep on haunting me to tears?
Am I bound like a slave
Unable to break free?

Or can I start the day anew
And make tomorrow mine?
With the hope that you hear
The prayers I sing to you.

I'll harvest what is true
in dreams that cannot end.
Our tomorrows will be held by you.

And realize my dreams
That I've kept through all these years.
In the fall of my life,
I love you.

II. Book of Others

DEAR GOD,

Letters to God

Dear God

Books of Prayer

II. Book of Others

by Ken Stearns

Forgiveness

Acceptance

Compassion

Forgiveness

Facing the past

Dear God,

Forgiveness. What haven't you taught us? You've given us a plethora of good examples and lessons in religion that are played out in life. How is it that this simple act, one totally in our control and in our best interest, can be so difficult?

Forgiveness among nations, races and peoples, friends, family, and lovers. The closer the relationship, the harder it is to find the courage. Why is it that such a burden—one that can destroy nations, end friendships, wreck families, and torture lovers—can be so hard to release?

Among all your gifts seemingly given only to us, forgiveness is powerful, inspiring. It's not a miracle but has the power of one.

What is it about holding on to memories? Is it the deep hurt, the betrayal, the words, the act? What binds the burden to us, wraps it around our soul, slowly constricting us? The bigger the hurt, the more the scars deepen with each breath as the memories play on repeat, until they're embedded and become one with our soul.

When someone close hurts us, the pain, is real and the damage can seem everlasting. If that person is in a position of trust, responsibility, power—someone whom we rely on and who we need to protect us—when they let us down, the cut goes deep. Even worse, if they cause us pain directly, we can carry it much deeper within us as a shield and as a weapon against them. Or if we need to love that person, such as a father or a mother, it can become guilt, and we blame ourselves.

Burying the hurt and pain only gives it power, holds us back in our relationships and our personal growth. Truly, there is no going forward when we are held hostage or feel damaged by our past. The hole is there, leaking love, trust, hope, commitment, honesty.

Forgiveness. Is it a path to true love? Is it what it means to truly love another? And what if that love can only be unlocked with unconditional relationships? No matter the wrong, we're able to wash it from our souls, thereby loving so openly, so fully committed that it overwhelms us and those we love, those around us.

Forgiveness seems such a weak place once it's given for nothing, yet it makes us profoundly powerful, untouchable. No sword, no word, no deed can hurt us. Our souls of love and kindness absorbing all.

Dear God, help me understand how to release forgiveness from my soul. I want to be able to forgive deeply and completely and, in that act, feel the connection with you to set my spirit free, to release everything that weighs me down and burdens my soul, what pains my heart tonight.

Forgiveness

Measuring the true impact

Dear God,

What, exactly, am I forgiving? Don't I need to know that first? How do I know what's been taken from me, the real hurt? I can count the loss, feel the pain, and know the damage. Should I care, should I measure its value? What does it truly matter now, today, in this moment? Why am I focused on what's happened in the past, what I've lost, what someone owes me? Isn't this them owning me, not owing me?

I know where I am in life, and this moment is only a snapshot. Yes, it is in many ways a summation of my past, my journey, but it doesn't necessarily reflect my direction and define who I am. By letting go of things in the past, they won't own me *or* owe me anything, and I get my freedom. The true impact of carrying around the negative things from our past—the weight of carrying all these emotions—what does that do to us, to those around us, to our ability to look ahead in life? Not letting go is far more painful than letting go.

I've been thinking a lot about this lately. I can think back on many situations where friends or family let an incident define their lives over several years. Seemingly caught in a vortex surrounded by the event, being replayed over and over with new versions of potential motives and future outcomes. Their anger boiling over like a poison, seeping out of their lives into those around them.

We find ourselves shying away from those relationships—even if we have compassion for the person—because the poison of the emotions leaks out to all aspects of their relationships. The expectations and the weight of carrying the load over time make the final outcome worse than the original damage.

Physical and emotional scars are all part of life, and how we deal with them each day forward is our choice, a reality we create. Carrying hate, anger, regret is a choice. My road in life has led me to this place. There is no right and no wrong at this point. How I manage it from here is solely dependent on me, on what I choose to focus my emotions and where I choose to put my efforts.

The more I think about this, the more it becomes clear to me that it's much better to release the past, no matter the cost. The only cost of what happened in the past is the cost of not moving forward. Yesterdays don't matter in our todays. Forgiveness erases all past pain and opens the way to acceptance.

We are in control of our lives, planning and acting toward who we want to become, and there's so much power in this idea. Focusing on the horizon has an immediate impact on our lives. As we move past thinking and begin doing things, we feel the power of manifestation giving us a tailwind—even *leading the way* at times—to a place we hadn't imagined.

Dear God, let me appreciate that the true impact of letting go and forgiving people from my past is the freedom it gives to me. Once I cut ties with this part of my past, I can focus on the present and the future. I can make my own path and not be defined by my past.

Forgiveness

Truly letting go

Dear God,

How does one truly let go? If someone has caused deep pain that's embedded in our souls—and we have forgiven them—how can we let go of the pain? How do we remove it from our minds, our souls, our consciousness?

How long we have carried the pain, the depth of it, and how much it has become a part of us will determine how challenging it will be to let it go. Truly forgiving—letting go of that painful thought and not letting it control us or our relationships—is where we want to go. Getting there is not easy.

Forgiveness is complex, and it's not linear. Forgiveness has multiple steps. Each one has its own experience, its own emotion, so truly letting go can be a process that may take a while. It's a cycle we'll need to repeat, from recognizing something from our past we want to confront to cleaning it out.

Still, it's not always a straight line, and each step can be more like peeling an onion, layer after layer, each one an experience or a process that's a bit different to resolve. And since it involves humans, relationships, life, it's often a matrix of onions, each with different layers. We can take the time to peel each layer and rationalize why it's good to let it go. Layer by layer, emotion by emotion. Step by step. This takes patience, resolve, courage. Forgiving and trying to let go of the pain feels like driving into a black hole of pain, stirring up memories, relationships, emotions.

This is when the healing begins, the growth. The whole point of forgiveness, letting go, is to move on in life, control your destiny, and this healing is an important step. To do that, we have to first truly let go and forgive, and be clear and complete so we can move forward. We're told that people who hurt us don't deserve forgiveness—it's too nice, too kind. Yet, carrying hate and anger with us as a badge of courage and self-righteousness is a far worse punishment—one we often choose for ourselves.

Imagine feeling weightlessness and euphoria. Imagine living without hate, anger and remorse, fear of the past, living without consciously inputting the past into each equation. All gone. Imagine no longer thinking or talking in a negative way about the past and having the freedom to think and talk and dream about the future. Truly letting go is all about growth, all about freedom, all that is within our control. Getting there is not easy, and the pain we must face to get there can be overcome when we focus on the outcomes of our freedom.

Dear God, thank you for the gift of free will—for the choice to truly let go. Give me the courage to change this part of my life. For the sake of the future that I don't know, help me to let go of the false security and comfort of this thing I hold on to. Give me this courage, this strength to cast aside what my past holds over me. Help me to rejoice in the freedom of the unlimited possibilities in the uncertainty of the future, and to rejoice in the certainty of being free of the past.

Forgiveness

Creating value

Dear God,

Why is it the best lessons in life, the ones that have the most impact on our lives, are often the most difficult to learn, the most wrought with pain? They shape who we are, who we have become. What is it about these peak life experiences that embeds them so deeply in our psyche? What creates our submission to let them define us?

If we have faced off with our past, measured the true impact of what we must forgive to move on in our lives, and found a way to truly let go, then here we are: Ready to find the value in life's experiences, recognize them as lessons to be learned, and carry them along with us in life.

There are few who can see our pain. But there is so much to be learned and carried forward—lessons from the pain and from the events themselves, the actions and the inaction, the words spoken and unspoken.

We learn who to trust and who not to trust, and when to trust ourselves and our instincts. Life's experiences make us more equipped to deal with the future, make us smarter, more composed, more savvy. Once we have gone through all the stages and packed up the valuable bits, an experience becomes a memory that's now transactional. We have paid some price and, in exchange, become better for it.

This exchange—converting a bad situation in life into a positive lesson—better arms us for life. It enriches our character, and as we overcome our past and our difficulties in life, we gain the trust and respect of those around us. Being able to manage life inspires confidence and trust in others. Finding the value in challenges, tragedies, bad situations and events is what makes us the most human. The human spirit is alive in this process. Truly we show what you, God, have intended for us to be: Adaptable and powerful enough to overcome whatever life gives us—and turn that experience into knowledge, into power.

I promise that I'll find a way to forgive, to let it go completely and find the good in the bad, to focus my energies on using the power of the lesson to lighten my way and push me forward. I promise not to get caught up in a cyclone of anger, hate, despair and disappointment.

I'll create value out of hurt and pain. I'll show others who have been wronged the way to let go, heal, and focus on looking forward. I'll show them how to take the lessons of their journey and leverage them, make the slave the master.

Dear God, show me the way as we forgive through strength, not forgetting. We are remembering so we can quantify the damage, measure the true impact, modulate how we react, and extract the maximum value to carry forward into our future as a shield against our past.

Acceptance

Bias, judgment, prejudice

Dear God,

There is so much hardwired bias and judgment built into us—a prejudicial need to group ourselves into tribes—that it takes enormous presence of mind, an awareness, to rethink and reframe situations as we go through life. We need to be aware of our pre-wired DNA—and use this awareness as a safety measure when looking at people's similarities and differences.

Only through this kind of awareness can we cast aside those hard-wired traits and replace them with a perspective of our own choosing. Instead, humanity tribalizes everything. We continue to work against each other and not for each other.

What animal does man have to fear, really? We are the top of the food chain. So why do bias and prejudice remain? Is it our instinctual open prairie, to kill or be killed, judging everything as a threat or a prey? This prejudice need not be carried anymore. We're past that in our evolution.

For what purpose do we need to label people? Broad differences that are demonized lead to smaller and smaller groupings, smaller tribes, until we have little in common. We're left with more reasons to hate each other and fight than to recognize what we share.

God, did you endow us with this shortcoming? We use the smallest differences—even among people of the same religion and same color as us—to discriminate with prejudice and hate, to tribalize, and even to kill each other. God, I am not talking about the ignorance around race or sexual orientation or politics. I'm speaking to the hardwired base-level scanning of people for things in common and, at the same time, for the differences. Fight or flight, friend or foe.

How do we control that process? How do we "hack" it? Instead of using it to narrow down a viewpoint, we should be using it to open up to a more accepting manner. How can we establish our own way to be open, inquisitive, balanced? The answer is clear: By removing our bias and simply understanding someone's perspective by listening, not judging, and affirming our understanding, showing our acceptance.

Understanding people as they are, without bias, without emotion, without judgment, is the first step to true acceptance. Accepting people allows us to fully understand them, their ideas, motives, ways. Being able to put aside our biases, our prejudices, and show our understanding gets us closer to people, allows for better understanding, puts us in a better position to make a sound judgment and have that judgment respected, as well.

What a powerful gift of acceptance and compassion that comes from this place. Balanced with our hardwired survival genes, which are instilled in all mammals, is the ability to turn them into strengths.

Dear God, give me the clarity to live without bias, to remember that only when we fully accept someone can we begin to understand them.

Acceptance

Acceptance and mirroring go hand in hand

Dear God,

You have given us the gift of seeing people without looking through a lens of color or race, country, creed, size, looks, DNA, or intelligence. You enable us to look *past their past*, accepting them for who they are at that moment, good or bad.

This gift of yours is so liberating, so empowering, and we are heartened by the good cheer and confidence we feel. Acceptance begets acceptance. Acceptance allows people to be open-hearted and to accept us for who we are, which is powerful. This simple act is tremendous. It liberates the person who extends the acceptance from the weight of judgment, and it empowers the person who receives the acceptance to be who they are and show what they are capable of.

If we put aside all of our preconceptions about people, we won't limit our view of the world with assumptions, labels, and bias. Tribalization is assigning people into groups, which is the opposite of acceptance. If we start with acceptance—pure acceptance—we learn who people are and what they do, believe in, and love and respect. Isn't true acceptance the absence of preconceived notions, ideas, labels?

In turn, when we really accept others, they, too, suspend judgment and accept us for who we are. Where we do not judge, we are likely not to be judged. So, if it is acceptance we seek, we should start with unconditional acceptance—including self-acceptance. This mirroring effect will allow us to fully accept ourselves. Being at peace with others leads to being at peace with ourselves.

The feeling of being accepted as I am and for who I am is limitless, inspiring. The impact of labels, biases, or prejudices on me is suffocating, but acceptance makes me feel empowered.

If I can find this kind of acceptance from those close to me and even from strangers, why can't I find the same acceptance from myself? Do I know myself too well? Am I too critical of myself? Only I know the real me, what I'm capable of, and what my dreams hold. But what am I truly willing to sacrifice to achieve what I can envision?

We can come to peace with ourselves, who we are, what we want to achieve and what we want to be in life. We can understand our faults, our shortcomings, and accept ourselves. But we should not expect approval when we don't do what's right and what's promised.

The same is true for others around us. We have to appreciate where they, too, want to be, who they want to be, and their struggle to get there. Even with what we might know of another person, we still pledge to accept that person as they are. We aren't forgetting. We aren't approving. But in this moment, we can accept, understand, and show compassion. From there, anything is possible.

Dear God, help me as I seek to accept myself. Let me find my self-love by accepting others, welcoming the diversity, seeking to understand. Help me to widen that net of acceptance, so all people can feel the love of others as well as the self-love, compassion, and understanding we all need.

Acceptance

Open your heart

Dear God,

Once we begin to accept people and they, in turn, accept us, as a consequence, we can accept ourselves more deeply—a meaningful connection opens a pathway to self-love. The feeling of being accepted touches our hearts and allows us to accept ourselves fully. That warm feeling is the power of your gift of love. In the end, the most important love is self-love, from which all other love proceeds. And self-love comes from accepting others.

Love opens our hearts even more than we thought possible—to being loved, feeling loved, and loving ourselves. Love both attracts and projects *more* acceptance and love.

Once all the pathways of acceptance are open, then we naturally open our hearts. And as we let ourselves become more vulnerable, we also become more comfortable with others. The emotional confidence that comes with acceptance is powerful.

An open, loving heart brings positive energy everywhere it travels.

It can warm a cold room and make a stranger a friend. We all know those people in our lives who are accepting, loving, self-loving—they open their hearts and joyously share their emotions and positive energy. A truly open and broadcasting heart pulls others into the warmth it creates.

An open heart can heal and bring joy, give forgiveness, acceptance, and compassion. The presence of a person with an open and warm heart is different. Their smile and their aura *scream* warmth and safety, comfort, love and kindness, acceptance, wisdom. It's inviting and healing. And why can't we have the same? It's all within our control. Through acceptance and the choices we make, we have the knowledge to get there—by letting people in, making ourselves vulnerable, by opening our heart.

We will share beautiful moments when we are navigating the waters of trusting others with our hearts; we will share growth and love. To be sure, opening our hearts will inevitably expose us to pain and hurt. But we'll find ourselves stronger each time—and able to manage the pain. Our hearts will open wider, bigger, committed to the idea.

When our hearts become black holes for love, we attract both the good and the bad, blending them together. Opening our hearts to loving others and allowing ourselves to be loved allows us and those around us to evolve together, morally and spiritually. Those who struggle to evolve are absorbed into the overwhelming good and become part of the experience. Once they gain momentum, the physics of open hearts produces endless energy.

Dear God, I want to open my heart. I've accepted people as they are, felt the connection of being accepted, and found self-love. I need the courage to open my heart, to make myself vulnerable, to balance the hurt and the pain with the anticipation of acceptance, a heart-to-heart connection.

Acceptance

Teaching others

Dear God,

Is it a burden or a blessing, when we know and understand what we see with an accepting, open and loving heart? It's not the same worldview as those who have closed hearts, are reluctant to accept others and, in the process, are judgmental. What a blessing to be able to truly see people and accept them for who they are, to feel accepted for who you are, and to accept yourself! The burden is knowing what others don't know. They can't see what we can see. They've gotten lost along the way and need help. We have to teach others and open their eyes to a different way. If they are already on a good path, then our responsibility is to enhance and reaffirm their approach.

Of course, we have to choose the path to teaching. We will begin to understand more deeply and to learn from another perspective—through the eyes of a guide, a teacher. We will never know what's coming next, and we may even be unaware of what the lesson means in the big picture, let alone at the moment. In that process of learning to teach are, of course, powerful experiences. We may see the outcomes and understand the power of the message—yet don't fully appreciate it.

Teaching others, giving of oneself, sharing knowledge and wisdom—these things are not a one-way street. We aren't giving anything away. We are harvesting our life experiences and sharing with others on an endlessly abundant journey.

Sharing is difficult, and each person has a lens through which to see the world, but the view is layered with the soot and grime of experience that has built up over the years. We trust in the present, and change is scary and risky. We can help people take off their lenses and see the world through their own, pure eyes, as a baby sees the world.

Then we can stand as an example of how it can be done. We can help them find their way to opening their own hearts, by being an example of the type of person we can all become.

God, if I can teach others to learn how to manage their yesterdays, live in and value today, and create an environment where tomorrows are a continual harvest, wouldn't that help many people? People can learn to better manage their relationship with themselves, become a better version of themselves.

If I can pass on knowledge about how to better get along with other people— teaching them forgiveness and acceptance—doesn't that multiply the effect? In their interactions with people, they can have a different outlook and improved relationships—with themselves and others.

Dear God, give me the spirit to share these ideas. Guide me on the way to meet the right people, to speak in the right way, and truly communicate. Let the value of the message inspire people to make a change.

Compassion

Truly understand the other person

Dear God,

What is compassion, really? What does it mean to be compassionate? I know instinctively that it's not crying at a picture of a starving child. That's an emotional reaction not related to a person's suffering. Isn't compassion something more? Don't we need to know the details of where our compassion should be directed and in what shape, what form? Isn't it about understanding people, living in their shoes, understanding why they are in their situations, and offering a helping hand and support that makes sense?

Understanding is an experience to be felt, touched, seen, involving all the senses.

We need to truly understand another person to get to a place of compassion. Certainly, having forgiving and accepting hearts puts us in that place. Showing our acceptance and forgiveness, and peeling away the layers of our defenses will allow others to become vulnerable and allow us to truly know and understand.

All people want to be understood, heard, respected and unjudged—but freely, on their own terms. Maybe it's been a long time since the person we're talking to has let anyone get this close. The level at which we interact with them has to be *human to human*. We must be accepting and non-judgmental, allowing all the truth, all the stories, all the mistakes, all the hurts, pains and anger to come out. We must walk side by side with people through this thing called life, listening to one another, seeking understanding, with respect, and without judgment.

When we open ourselves to other people like this, and they to us, the moment can be powerful. We may share little in common, going in different directions from different places, but for one, shining moment, those two souls will connect and grow that day.

Only when our souls touch can we understand. When someone feels our acceptance, it opens the pathway to vulnerability. This takes us deeper and deeper into their truth, opening up new layers and new truths.

What else can we do, God? Share our own journeys? Successes, failures, our own mistakes, the pain we have caused and the pain we have endured? There must be value in their understanding us as we understand them. Sharing my journey would show the vulnerability I am comfortable with, the confidence in myself and the outcomes I can manage.

Give us confidence. Let us understand each other first. Give us the willingness to come to people's sides, listen, understand, and then share our story as well. Let them open up and share more.

Dear God, let me sit side by side with people at the time when they really need to be heard and understood, when they need a compassionate person to care and love.

Compassion

360-degree view of someone else

Dear God,

Once I know someone as a person—sitting side by side and sharing, opening our hearts, trying to make sure I understand him and he understands a little bit about me—don't I need to really listen to his story from his side now, from his eyes? Not as a friend with endearing compassion but as living his experiences through him, fully appreciating his situation, feeling what he feels, aligning as best I can with his point of view.

Getting someone to open up at this level and walking with him down this pathway to vulnerability, we really need to commit to listening, understanding the situation: the who, what, when, how, and why. Feeling what he feels from the inside out, and then farther, outside the body, to how he has interacted with the world.

See his life experience, right or wrong, non-judgmentally, without pity, but understanding. Not just a static linear life journey, but 360 degrees so we understand the whole picture.

From somewhere in life, he came this way. His interaction with the world, the back and forth, the feeling, and how he got to this place at this moment. Let's find his way back out the way he came. Understanding someone from the inside out enables us to share his emotions. Without that, compassion is not fully felt by the giver or the receiver. But once someone feels that we really know his situation, anything is possible.

Imagine that "a-ha!" moment when we realize how someone got here, the event that started a process. The tipping point, if you will. If we can truly understand how someone came to this point in need—from his perspective—then we can understand that moment. We can share together and agree together, "Yeah, that was a big moment." Shining a light on that, using that as a center point from which to grow the conversation.

If someone knew my toughest moments that intimately, he would be someone with whom I would trust to take the next steps. We can use this as a bridge to explore more life experiences, find more life events people need to work through, forging deeper into the relationship and the 360-degree level of understanding for true compassion.

Showing our acceptance, increasing our level of understanding where a person is today, can only lead to better understanding the root causes so we can help. Ultimately, compassion is about helping someone out of his situation.

Dear God, grant me the patience to have an open heart, open ears, and attentive eyes to listen deeply and truly to people. Let them open their hearts to me, so I can connect with them, and truly and deeply understand them.

Compassion

Understanding core needs, the root cause

Dear God,

I know that this all sounds so logical in my head, but I know that, with people, things are never straightforward and always more complex than I can imagine. Still, we need to follow the logical next step and understand why someone is in a situation. Not try to treat the symptoms. That's not compassion. That's pity.

Like when a heavy drinker has health issues and goes to the doctor. What's the problem? The health issues? The drinking? *Why* is he drinking? To escape what?

Compassion isn't just feeling a bond, an understanding, and enabling a fix around some symptoms. Sure, it's not easy to get this far, but there is a chance to do greater things here through understanding the root cause of someone's situation. Even he might not be aware of how and why he is where he is.

Getting to the real causes is not linear. They are layered, like an onion. The deeper to the core a person goes, the more powerful the memories, the sharing, and the pain. But closer to the truth, the root cause, lies the solution.

Compassion is the process of understanding someone, his situation, how and why he got there, and how to help him. Uncovering each issue, each cause—how many minor causes we have to face, solve, and nurture before we can find the real cause—peels the onion away. Looking for the root cause takes time and commitment, a commitment to the individual and the outcome.

People put up many layers of defense to hide the truth, hide the real feelings, defend their raw emotions, their real pain. Are they embarrassed, shy? Does it hurt too much? Will the truth hurt someone else? Do they hide the truth from themselves? Isn't this what most of us do—bury the most painful truths the deepest?

Even the person we would be helping may not know the real root cause. He might have forgotten or buried it, or not realized its impact. So, the discovery together is powerful. What a huge emotional release for this person.

Getting to the root cause, peeling the onion, is the only way to truly understand how to help someone. Getting there is not easy. We get to the discovery through compassion.

Dear God, give me the insight, the wisdom, the strength to work with someone in pain, someone in need. Help him to peel away the years of defense, come to terms with the real issues in his life, solve those problems holding him back, help him leverage the lessons and move on in life. And give me the strength to help him get there.

Compassion

One step, one helping hand, one push, one follow-up

Dear God,

Isn't there more to compassion than simply understanding the other person? Can we really examine a person's whole life—his history, his pains and suffering, failures, hurts and anguish—find the root cause, and then leave him alone to manage?

Shouldn't we take the first step forward and offer helping hands up? Reach out with open hands, open hearts, take people under our wing and comfort them, give them the courage to face the way forward and take their own first steps? We can only do so much, and at some point, they need to walk their lines to self-determination. But helping them take their first steps—that can come from us. We have been on this path before, we know the way. We can take their hands.

Understanding the real issues in someone's life, the reasons behind them, and feeling and sharing the compassion associated with that discovery is powerful. Then extending a hand to someone who knows that we truly understand, and taking that first step together are so powerful.

Pushing someone to change his situation, supporting him, challenging him, and following up is true compassion. It's what separates compassion from pity. With the power of true compassion, past forgiveness and past acceptance, we can go much deeper by opening our arms, our hearts, minds, and souls.

But compassion doesn't end there. Helping someone resolve his truths, plan his way ahead, helping him take that first step is the beginning. There are many first steps. Some end in success and some in setback. We stay connected, follow up, ensure that progress is there on the road to where he wants to be.

Everyone, no matter his state, is capable of hope. Understanding where that person is and lending a helping hand to take the first step, and then pushing him with compassion to do his best to try one more time, puts hope before despair, belief in place of doubt. And prayer will sustain our efforts, our minds, our hearts.

Dear God, help me find the strength to take these last steps. Let

the compassion of helping others give me strength and courage to take their hands and lift them up, help them to stand and to take their first steps.

III. Book of All

Letters to God

Dear God

Books of Prayer

III. Book of All

by Ken Stearns

Love

Karma—Chart a course

Service—Giving back

Love

Loving yourself

Dear God,

What is love? Truly, of all the blessings you bestow upon your creation, none is more beautiful, empowering, inspiring—yet debilitating, destructive, wicked.

Love's intangible yet has the power to build and destroy nations. Bring people together, and tear them apart. Heal wounds we cannot see, and scar so deeply we feel we can never recover.

Where does it exist? Is it in our heads as a kind of emotion we create, or is there a chemical reaction when we feel we are in love? Could it be an organ inside our bodies that we have yet to fully understand, or does it reside in our souls and this is why we truly can't see or understand it?

If it's in my soul, what does that mean? Am I a sum of all my love, good or bad, through the life I have lived? Do I carry the full quantity with me and reconcile it with you when I pass through this life on my way home to you?

Don't we view love all wrong? Put our love onto someone else, our focus of love onto other people, without nurturing and ensuring that self-love is there?

Love is an emotion that's inside out. To love, to truly love, you must love yourself first. Of course, acceptance, compassion, forgiveness must be there, but looking in the mirror, you should feel love, happiness. Eye to eye in the mirror, with the longest stare, we should look deep into our eyes, deep inside, and see the details, the reflections, reach the soul. We need calm and a quiet confidence in our self-love.

Who knows us better than ourselves? Our own minds constantly judge us, our thoughts, our deeds; what we felt here, what we did or didn't do here and there. We know what we are capable of and what we give to life, and the struggle we face in discovering ourselves is certain to cause us to judge ourselves and measure ourselves along our path.

Against our own expectations, we disappoint ourselves. So how can we forgive ourselves for being imperfect and human, with a compassion to understand that, for all the gifts, the struggle is real and constant, conflicted and unintentional? Help us, God, to find in our hearts a love for ourselves, a deep compassionate love and acceptance for who we are, the current version of ourselves. For sure, we plan how to grow into a better version, but today we must love who we are, as is, with all our heart, accepting, forgiving, free from yesterdays. Love today, now, and forever, and mean it.

Loving myself is such a powerful thing. It's within my reach and in my own control. And with it, I can learn to love others, truly, deeply, without judgment. A purity that can be seen and felt, understood. Self-love is the most powerful gift we have—and the most useful in learning to love others.

Dear God, I can only imagine the power, the freedom and liberation that come once someone truly accepts himself, loves himself wholly, purely, deeply. Self-acceptance, forgiveness, and compassion touch and heal one's own soul, warms the heart, clears the mind. I truly believe love starts here.

Love

Loving others

Dear God,

Self-love is the foundation from which love builds its strength—it's radiating and warm, an envelope of confidence.

With the foundation of loving oneself, loving others is possible. When we are at peace with ourselves and love ourselves, others can feel that our bodies' and souls' vibrations are signaling an harmonic unity. Love can release chemicals we don't understand, heal wounds we cannot see. So, when we open our heart to someone, offering our love, it's powerful, magnetic. It's pure.

There are so many shapes and sizes of love, so many variants and manifestations. The love between a young couple, or the love a mother and a father have for their children. The love when newborns see their mothers for the first time. When we see the embodiment of love in a baby's gentle, innocent face, we know love is not taught, earned, bartered for, promised. It's but a deep connection, hardwired, an unspeakable bond.

This moment when two souls gaze upon each other, they momentarily become one, leaving behind some piece with each other, some aura, some shared sense of connection, like a string that stretches across time, distance, and space. Over time the depth and strength of love can grow, the connection grows, strengthens—at the same time growing more and more elastic—as love is an emotion and not bound by time or space.

Learning to extend love, true love, past oneself to others takes time; love is a journey, often one we need to restart, trying, trying again. It takes time, maturity, but it's so worth it. Love for others is not bound by time, events, and place, and its effects go past our life, past their lives and our time together. Love lasts. True deep love once felt and experienced doesn't just feel good. It changes one's chemistry, binds us to another soul, yet frees both our souls, heals our souls.

From the safe harbor of being loved unconditionally by our loving soul, one that accepts and loves without judgment, then another can be free to explore the most fearful things, the biggest challenges, climb the highest mountain alongside the strength of our love and belief and acceptance, no matter the outcome.

Love is powerful. We can heal people with it, or we can hurt people with it. Love is always in short supply and high demand. Although we may not always see people in need, they are there, around us—even those closest to us.

Dear God, My love for my daughters never fades, and no matter time or distance, my heart fills with their emotions of pain, my whole being fills with their joy. Let my Love for others mirror the love of family, a connected love that extends beyond time and space.

Love

Accepting love

Dear God,

How is it possible to feel loved, accept love, if one hasn't truly accepted himself, learned to love himself, or learned to love others? We need to be loved, feel loved, know that someone is there. But what if, no matter how much someone loved us and filled that one need, deep inside there's truly a hole? What if accepting love was not possible? Love was appreciated, enjoyed, but not absorbed or nurtured.

What a difficult and challenging feeling, being loved when we haven't gotten to the place of self-love or loving others. Others can and will love us. But absorbing, feeling that warmth, and accepting the powerful emotion of another soul's energy, its blue electric light enveloping ours, is impossible if our own energy is on another frequency or our antenna is shut down.

This is why it's so important to get to a place of self-love first.

What an amazing feeling love is. Nothing can equal it. Connected to another—with both people loving him or herself—where each can accept and feel full love in a reciprocal way. The sound of our name can elevate our physical and emotional state. The words "I love you" can bring about the sensations of warmth, calm, and excitement—all at the same time.

One of the great joys of parenthood is the full acceptance of love. Children soak it up. They grow from it, and they need it like air and water. In their pure hearts, they seek love as their anchor in life, their security and safety. Being loved, accepting love, and loving others is the way we are born, but we drift away from that anchor over time.

Why is it that we forget our childlike and innocent love as we grow up, a love so positive, so binding and unconditional? Later in life, we fall in love, and when that love fails, we feel a pain that seemingly can't be healed, only to try again in search of an eternal connection, a love that heals all our losses, gives us strength and confidence to conquer the world. No matter the number of times we love and hurt, we will always be searching for that matching frequency and that love that supports us, builds us.

There's power in loving ourselves and accepting love from others—that feeling of opening our hearts, letting love in, becoming vulnerable. There's power in the emotion of accepting and binding as one with another—two souls in harmony, freely exchanging love, harmonized in frequency. Pure joy.

Dear God, Let me abandon my fears, my vulnerabilities, and my doubts, and let love in. Truly open my heart through loving myself, and help me connect with others by accepting their love with all its joy and pain.

Love

Teaching love

Dear God,

Loving myself, loving others, accepting love—how can I not share this? This inward healing that I feel from loving myself and loving others close to me. The brightness in my aura, the glow, the energy as my friends, loved ones, and family feel the power of my pure, unjudging love. Not by the words "I love you" but by the warmth of my soul that comes from my own acceptance and love of self. Is there a purity of love that, once I've found it, others can feel?

What begins as an emotion evolves into something truly felt, transferred between two people. How does one move from a fragile emotion that's full of its own doubts, pains, and elations to a fully transferable feeling of love? Can love be felt, communicated with the touch of a hand? With the look of an eye, can I touch another's soul with my gaze?

Having found how to love ourselves and others and accepting that love is hard, rare, and amazing. Our burden becomes spreading that knowledge, helping others to understand. It's a burden of joy, peace, completeness.

When we touch someone with our love, it recharges his body, stimulates his mind, and heals his soul. It electrifies his karma. You can see a physical change in his appearance immediately. He moves to the next appointment, chore, task with a euphoric aura, beaming. This power of love one feels.

But how does one teach love? There is no class in school, no major. There is no profession that educates people on something this important and fundamental—in *being good humans*. All religions that look up to you, God, teach love and the different kinds of love, yet today so many of us struggle with self-love as a first step.

Helping people learn to love themselves cleanly with an open and pure heart is such a powerful place to start. Of course, it begins with us accepting them. We need to forgive them, if needed, and have the compassion to see where they are in their lives and how they got there. Then we need to rally the courage to take the first step to help them, to help them learn how to love themselves, to appreciate where they are in life and who they are.

Teaching someone else to extend that loving acceptance toward others is an easy next step, but the real test comes when we ourselves become vulnerable and open our own hearts and accept love—as well as the emotions and the responsibility that come with it. Teaching this is profound. It will leave both the student and teacher impacted, bonded, tethered in life.

Dear God, I need the strength to keep my self-love alive and strong and my love with others healthy. For me, for them. I need the wisdom to guide others to self-love and on to sharing this gift with others. Show me the way.

Love giveth

Love giveth, love taketh
Love makes us, or breaks us
Love builds us, it destroys us
When you love someone, you gotta love yourself

I fell in love with the girl next door, so young
I never felt that way before,
My heart pounded like a drum, she had me under her thumb,
She was perfect in every way, auburn hair and those green eyes
But she crushed my soul when she walked away
Oh, baby, love never was the same

Love giveth, love taketh
Love makes us, or breaks us
Love builds us, it destroys us
When you love someone, you gotta love yourself

I met a lovely girl in school, she played me for the fool
I chased her hard and won her heart
Took her to the dance and to see mom and dad
Got her on the boat where we said "I do"
We had two kids, it was all too much
Compromise and alibis weren't enough to save my soul

Love giveth, love taketh
Love makes us, or breaks us
Love builds us, it destroys us
When you love someone, you gotta love yourself

The harder I loved, the harder I fell
The more I gave love, the more it took from me
As people loved me, so reckless I was, for being loved, betraying love
I wasn't careful with their hearts, I hurt their souls, now here I am alone

The fall of my youth, spring of my winter
Having learned in the end loving myself is all that matters

Love giveth, love taketh
Love makes us, or breaks us

Karma—Chart a course

Every action

Dear God,

What is karma? Is it the sum of my good deeds measured against all the times I did wrong, the net total of my treatment of the world during my journey through this life? Is it small stuff, big stuff? Sometimes it seems I should improve my thinking about all possible things that contribute to my karma. Does my karma begin with my thoughts and end with the consequences of my deeds? I mean, it can't be just the acts themselves; what's in my heart and my mind must count, too.

What if karma is an energy that's created by our thoughts and actions? The positive things we do and think make strong vibrations that harmonize at beautiful, calming frequencies, while the bad acts dampen and suppress our vibrations, tuning us into a negative energy. We are broadcasting either a positive or a negative karma. Is this why I find I'm drawn to certain people, while, with others, I don't want to be in the same room?

When we create positive energy—meaning well-intentioned,

loving, and kind actions—it will have a multiplying positive effect. And the impact is beyond what we see. Exactly the opposite is happening when we do things wrongly or intentionally hurt people. It reverberates and pushes past the intended act. The measurement, the karma's impact, has to be understood in order to help people accept responsibility and give enough evidence to change.

The more positive actions we take in life, with ourselves and with those around us, the more we inspire and attract others who create positive things. And once we understand the power of karma—how far it reaches and its long-term impact both good and bad—then we can really help people change.

Imagine the law of attraction and Newton's laws working together and applied to a view that's not about the physical world but about our actions, words, and thoughts. We will see those actions in the vibrations they create and their effect on others around us.

Being a good person and doing the right thing heals, binds, and strengthens quietly, without fanfare or fame, while spreading that kindness and love far past its intended recipient. It's perhaps a different view or an understanding—a measurement, if you will—of good and bad, a *human* approach.

Dear God, Every word and deed has some energy behind it, negative or positive. We do need some balance, but, certainly, we want to be a positive-energy-emitting force. Help me be that force.

Karma—Chart a course

Golden rule plus

Dear God,

In how many ways and into how many cultures have you sown the maxim: Do unto others as you would have them do unto you. Across religions, languages, and the centuries. There's such tremendous power in that, it's survived thousands of years.

The idea of treating people the way we expect to be treated focuses on people's basic expectations. But what if we were to go beyond that—what if we were to strive to treat people better than they expect? Wouldn't it have a powerful effect on them, and then on others? Is the effect exponential?

The better you treat others, the greater the impact. Can we treat everyone we come in contact with a little better than we would like to be treated? Just a bit more effort here and there? Kinder, more heartfelt. A warm smile when we greet someone, or a "Thank you" with eye contact and saying his name. Not random acts of kindness here and there, but naturally treating the people you meet every day with just a little bit more effort in the human touch.

When I was in college, I had a job as a bartender. The salary was low, so I worked for tips. In that situation, I gave service far greater than a customer would expect, hoping to increase my cash for the night. I exceeded the Golden Rule every night with every transaction. Delivering great service, smiling, trying.

I managed my expectations, however, knowing that while most people would take care of me, some would not even tip. It's the reality of service work. Still, it was disappointing when I went the extra mile and my customer didn't recognize or appreciate my efforts. When it hurts, we often spread that pain to colleagues. Conversely, I recall the moments when I was tipped beyond my expectations and how it elevated my mood, my emotions. I couldn't keep that to myself and outwardly shared the joy, the experience, the feelings.

The real lesson isn't that it's nice to treat each person kindly. It's about how going past the level he expects changes his behavior and how the effect multiplies. When we make the effort, show the care and respect, and exceed a person's expectations in a personal and compassionate way, the impact is exponential. He will quickly share his joy—and with more than one person.

***Dear God, Let me feel and show the power of the human touch through my words, actions, and thoughts. Help me focus on treating everyone just a little bit better than he imagines and know the impact it makes on him, someone close to him, and—somehow*—on me.**

Karma—Chart a course

Measure and change where we are

Dear God,

What's the way forward now that I am aware of karma, of my words and my actions? Where do I begin, and where am I now? Shouldn't I know where I stand? I am committed to changing. I've always been conscious of the idea of karma but never set my mind to practice a life toward improving.

How did I do today? Did I treat people in the same way I want to be treated? Even better? Was I thoughtful and courteous, kind in my words and polite in my actions? Did I look people in the eye and use their names? Striving to finish each day in the positive is a good direction.

I'll just start with today—then each day is all that I can change, one by one. Being aware that this is something we should do, something we *can* and *should* change. Just knowing and thinking about it is a great step. While we can't change the past, going forward, we can act in a more positive way.

God, I do wonder. What's the sum of my interactions with others, and what's the sum of all our frequencies, of all our actions—negative *and* positive. In this life, how many days have I ended in the positive and how many in the red? What does my scorecard look like? What's my net karma?

Should we care, can we change it, should we dwell on the realization that we might have a negative balance? Should we rest easily feeling we have done too much already? Is karma only one of life's scorecards? Are we carrying around many life balance sheets, a summation of our time as souls, carrying our karma from one life to the next, allowed to ascend to the highway of souls only when we achieve a perfect balance?

And then, shouldn't we do as much as we can in this life? Is the key to life here on Earth the secret to everlasting life? Life with others is so simple: Treat them the same way you want be treated. And, when possible, give a little bit more.

Dear God, If the key to eternal life and peace by your side is as

simple as treating others the way we want to be treated, then please give me the strength to live each day treating people better than they expect. All day, every day.

Karma—Chart a course

The manifestation

Dear God,

It really isn't enough to be aware, to commit to change, to focus on being a better person, is it? It has to be harder than that. It's about *living the life, the behavior* of the person we want to be, the one we can be, we all can be. It's about being the best human we can be here on this Earth in this life to each other and to all things.

This sounds good and makes sense. But how? I know for me it takes more. I need to manifest change—the new things in my life that I want to stay, to perpetuate, and make an impact. I want to manifest who I want to be, not who I am.

Manifestation requires me to be that person. Live the life, act as the person I aspire to be. This helps integrate the ideas, thoughts, and behaviors into my person, my life, and then into the people around me.

Change is not easy. Change is hard. Changing—no, *controlling*—my mind is the hardest part. But working through my mind, the better words will come. The power of my mind will set the direction, and better words will direct my actions. What I think and do will manifest who I want to become.

But the changes are not just to our thoughts, deeds, and words. The impact is greater than what we experience physically or emotionally. The physical change that we can't see is at a molecular level, the vibrations we emit. Steady, powerful, healing.

The process of changing does make us maybe not *a different person* but certainly one who gives off a much different feeling and attitude to be around. We will notice a shift in the kind of people we are now more attracted to.

Our energy changes, and its main benefit is the shift in the frequency at which we broadcast. This positive energy is more harmonic, travels rhythmically with ease, and we will more likely align with other people following the same path.

Dear God, Help me harness the power of my faith and embrace the manifestation of treating others as I would want to be treated. Help me live it daily and be the embodiment of that person I want to be.

Service—Giving back

Serve from where you are in life

Dear God,

I often wondered why churches took donations in even the most remote of places. Even in the poorest townships, they pass the offering plate, and almost inversely to their wealth, across the world, people *give*. The Church knows, the Mosque knows, the Temple knows. People are good. The poorest, those closest to suffering and at the edge of meeting their basic needs, give what they can as they appreciate the realities of life. Knowing they somehow have more than another, they embrace the value in giving.

Somewhere deep down in our beings, we long to help others. It's in there. I know it's there, and it's not parental; it is helping another human in time of distress and need. No matter our place in life, rich or poor, we have an opportunity to help others—no, we have a *need*, a *willingness*, and a *desire* to help others. Whether it's our time, our thoughtfulness, a helping hand, a kind word, a spoken or a written advocacy on behalf of a person in need—it doesn't matter, because all service makes a difference.

The easiest way to feel like we are doing something is by giving money and supporting others who are making it their life to help others. It's a powerful tool—but it's not the only measure of service.

Service can be done regardless of socio-economic class, culture, or creed. We can serve from where we are, close to home, widening our circle as we can. Service itself is a currency, so volunteering our time, ideas, and support are all hard currencies in life.

But sometimes, from where we are, all we can offer is a kind word, a warm look, a courtesy, touching one life at that moment. Small deeds from those with less can be as impactful as a large financial deed from someone with more. Person-to-person heartfelt help—a touch and a kind word—are so impactful to both the giver and the receiver.

This first step is so much about mind change, a mind shift. If we are to become service-minded, then actively looking for those opportunities needs to become part of our daily life. The consciousness of service creeps into the waking mind.

Dear God, Remind me every day that giving back is relative to where I am in life. Remind me that service comes in so many forms and never needs to be large or grand.

Service—Giving back

Start with the smallest step

Dear God,

I know I can help. I have an open heart, a compassionate heart. But how do I start? Should I go my own way or follow the path of organizations? Is it big stuff or small stuff that matters? Wouldn't starting small make the most sense, one person to one person, soul to soul?

Something close to home can lift up community members through local resources and knowledge. The impact of their help is much more valued, pertinent. Don't small changes in our lives earn an "Amen," and aren't they easier to make than big ones?

When I was a child growing up in the Midwest, I watched my father give money each Sunday at church. It helped support the local charities we had adopted over the years. I remember the terrible famines in Africa, and some of the images used to raise money were such difficult ways to see humanity. But service and charity were something far away, something we mailed in, we outsourced, something we handed to a third party. We kept away from the people we were meant to help.

When I got older, my mom and her women's group would do service work called Meals on Wheels, which delivered hospital meals to home-bound seniors in the area. Three times a week at lunchtime, cars would line up and receive about ten meals each, along with addresses. I joined Mom a few times because she'd pick me up on the half-days we attended then in early high school.

And it left a mark on me. Old age was real and often lonely. Surgeries and sicknesses leave people vulnerable and alone, and often in pain, unkempt almost always. Souls, humans, crave contact with others; it's not a drug—it's a food.

Every doorbell we rang, every smile we got warmed my heart. The thank-you's, the small talk I watched Mom engage in. But in the end, it broke my heart. To this day, when I think about it, it makes me cry. Loneliness is real. It's painful and close by, and preventable. I learned that the biggest impacts, the fastest and the easiest to maintain, are one-to-one, close, and in our community.

The most important work is next door or on the next street over, but not much farther away. It's easiest to deliver because it's so close and familiar.

It becomes more a way of life, more so than a kind of service that would require us to take time out or to plan for an event. It becomes part of our daily life. Little steps here and there, one touch, one smile, one helping hand, one kind word.

The bigger and the more complex, the more challenging it is to start and the more challenging to measure, to maintain, and to see and feel the impact. The more challenging to truly touch a soul. Service never needs to be grand.

Dear God, Let me take care of the people closest to me. No matter how small the effort, help me to find a way to say "Yes," a way to offer without being asked. Help me take the first step.

Service—Giving back

Return what you borrowed

Dear God,

Doesn't service really mean to give back, giving back what has been borrowed, what has been lent? We start our lives with nothing, and we finish with nothing. In today's world, life has never been better for people. We all start out with so much more than our ancestors. So much is taken for granted, everything is expected, and there is no such thing as too much of what we want and what we need.

The things that we have earned came with the cost of an initial investment somewhere along the way. We have taken the loans of life—we borrowed wisdom, food, care, education, love. The investments made in us benefit us, and we should enjoy what we have done well with. Yet, we should also recognize the debt we owe to the world around us.

Even if we have no wealth, and even if we are poor, we have wisdom, we have life experiences, we have a heart, we have our ears to listen to someone's story. We can comfort another, hold in our arms the body of a broken soul.

There are so many ways to give back and give service when you look at it this way. From the possessions we cannot take with us after this life to the knowledge from life's lessons, our beliefs, our courage, grit, humility, understanding: all are so valuable and easy to give away, yet are so carelessly held and shared so miserly.

How much should we be aware of our balance as we go through life? Have we returned what we borrowed, what was lent? If we borrow something, don't we owe interest as well as the principal?

Directly or indirectly, we give everything away the day we leave this Earth. We might pass on material wealth, but the greatest value will be buried with us if we don't pass on and share our knowledge, wisdom, and experience.

Isn't this where we *all* can be rich? We are all millionaires, owning many thousands of different types of experiences.

My greatest legacy, my greatest living benefit lies in passing on what I've learned. The mistakes I've made and what lessons they taught me, experiences with my family, and experiences alone, the many regrets and mistakes. What can't we share as we get older, and who isn't older than someone else?

Dear God, We all have so much to share from where we are. Even a five-year-old has wisdom to give to the two-year-old sibling. Help me serve, help me return what I have borrowed along the way.

Service—Giving back

Build your service, invest for returns

Dear God,

How do big charities stay in place for so long when their sole purpose is to serve? How do they keep going? How do they perpetually sustain themselves? Large organizations, large infrastructures require enormous resources to sustain themselves, to function. So, as we start out small, shouldn't we build a perpetuity into our service, one that's without a structure, one that self-generates, regenerates, and multiplies?

There are so many people in our communities who need some kind of help—attention, food, skills, love. Up and down the economic chain. Different needs at different levels.

Service can happen at every level of society, matching compassionate people with people in need. It makes sense. Time, thoughtfulness, neighbors helping neighbors, friends checking on friends, a web of service.

Think how empowering it is once we remove the barriers to service.

It's not about money. It's about connecting with people at the most basic level: rich or poor, educated or not, young or old—everyone needs something.

If we think of service without currency, without an infrastructure, charities, or seasons, what else can we change? The smallest help from the poorest and the most vulnerable is more valuable than the richest man's money.

As we do our service in life, is it something we can replicate, or something the recipient can replicate? If we find a way to serve society, it should be replicated, taught to others, and self-sustained into perpetuity.

Dear God, Help me find a way to build my service to others. Help me create a self-generating service that teaches others how to serve—from no matter where they are—and how to pass it on in life.

IV. Book of You

DEAR GOD,

Letters to God

Dear God

Books of Prayer

IV. Book of You

by Ken Stearns

Faith

Hope

Prayer

Faith

In the absence of proof

Dear God,

Isn't faith believing in something we can't see, touch, or hear? What drives us to put our trust and hope in something we can't hear from directly, see with our own eyes, or touch with our hands? This is a gift that only humans possess. We can believe in something intangible. We can act on the intangible. Put our life's meaning into a belief. Process the words, the promise, into belief and then action. We know there is more to life than can be explained, or even if so, understood.

Aren't we driven by our need to grasp how we got here and why our life matters? Human thinking. This search for our meaning, our inception leads us to you. But to get to the answers of why we're here on Earth like this, and for what purpose, we fall deep into the idea that this galaxy and beyond is intelligent in design. It's Godly, not accidental. We are here, we are special.

And in the absence of proof, we have faith.

It's the foundation of religion. It kindles hope and trust and love. It ends the darkness of doubt, hate, mistrust and must be kept lit in the darkest hours, the wickedest of storms. There will come a time when what divides us will matter little, and only our faith in humanity will remain.

God, is it time now that I trust my faith in you and trust my faith in myself? Knowing that, above all else, things will be all right? Isn't this the essence of faith? Marching forward, you by my side, holding my hand.

The strength of my faith. Faith in myself. Faith in your trust in me and your unconditional love. Letting go of all my fears, all my doubts, with a belief that there is something bigger than what I can see, what I can touch. More of what I feel in my soul. Drawing on that, the power, the confidence, it creates my faith in the absence of proof.

Things that I cannot explain but that I feel empower me and give me strength beyond my size, courage beyond my confidence. My faith in you translates to your faith in me, then builds my faith in myself. And once I have faith in myself, the conviction only grows in what I believe, what I do, how I love. My faith is in your guiding hands. My faith is in your plans. My faith is in your love.

This power of my faith—my faith in you and yours in myself—propels me toward my dreams, my goals. My destiny. It's out there, in your Universe. The connectivity of all things ensures it will happen.

Dear God, with my faith embraced, an aura surrounds me, envelops me like a protective bubble, impenetrable. I march on every day with you by my side. Setbacks today, scar tissue tomorrow, more stories to tell, one more challenge today, one less tomorrow.

Faith

Not without doubt

Dear God,

We can have faith in the absence of proof, but a faith that is a blind faith without challenge is itself dangerous. We must challenge our faith. Prove it, test it, validate it. Its cause, purpose, intent. And not without doubt.

Why give us the ability to make faith a tangible belief, and at the same time enable us with creative brains that are also logical, with critical thinking and problem solving? When there is an absence of proof, the human mind goes to work to solve this puzzle. There are doubts at times, and inevitably, we can be attacked by many.

Is the secret to faith the strength that's created by the forging, over and over, of the tenets of our faith? Challenges that arise one after another, whether external to one's faith or the internal dialogue of constant questioning?

Reinforcing our beliefs validates our faith, gives it strength, gives it purpose. And with a purpose, anything is possible. When you challenge your own faith and test it, this is where it is forged into your beliefs. A belief that is never tested is simply a hope by itself, a dream, a fantasy which cannot stand the challenges of life or the tests of time.

In the cycle of challenging and understanding and challenging again (but deeper), we forge a clearer and more comprehensive understanding and appreciation for our faith.

And we learn what's important about the faith we have in ourselves. It's a discovery process, and the best tool is to challenge your beliefs, resolve those challenges, and probe again—but wider and deeper. Challenge after challenge. Like a blacksmith making the finest blades, layering the steel, melting, hammering, folding, hammering, over and over again, forging together stronger and stronger bonds.

What is born out of the process of faith? A challenge, a test, a deeper understanding, a strengthening of beliefs. I am more confident, stronger, more aggressive in my works, focused on the outcomes, driven toward the ways that are best.

I am beginning to appreciate where the faith in myself is coming from, why I believe in the outcomes I want. I am prepared. I have challenged my faith in me, examined the plans, prepared and refined my edges. I believe in myself—but only after I have tested my beliefs in me. I labored to remove doubts, self-doubt, and made the preparations in my mind for what outcome I wanted, and then I put trust into those preparations. Faith, trust is prepared.

Dear God, test my faith in you and my faith in myself. Take me to the darkest corners, and strengthen my beliefs, my resolve. Confirm my direction, my plans. I'll emerge stronger, more confident, refined.

Faith

Believing in something bigger

Dear God,

When I was young, the concept of you was mind-boggling, an intangible, omnipresent, invisible being, creator of everything. As I grew older, my understanding grew. I better understood the world, the universe, and the galaxy, and I began to question everything. As I pass the fall of my life, I can see more clearly now what you have created — how big, how everlasting, yet impermanent, while remaining perfect in design and balance.

My whole understanding of you was once too narrow, too small. We must open our minds to something bigger than our definition of who we think you are.

If I were to live another 100 years, what would be my knowledge and capacity to appreciate, articulate, and interpret a new level of understanding be, what all this means? The first 50 years of my life I was asleep. Even awake for the next 100, my ability to comprehend may still fall behind the truth. *What will the next 25 reveal?* I wonder. I believe in this now — an infinite-by-all-measures omni-verse, a universe, galaxy, world, community. This realization is a wake-up call.

We should take not a “helicopter view” or even lunar view of the Earth and what lies here. Instead, move further away in the galaxy and beyond. All of it is infinite and expanding. Even an imploding giant galaxy that’s dying is but a speck among the infinite and expanding life created.

When we go through the process of finding faith without proof, challenging those beliefs, seeing that the design is for us to find faith in ourselves, believing we can be anything and do anything and are, in fact, limitless, within this infinite expanding interdependent space, we, too, become infinitely expanding. Our DNA is linked to and built into the universe.

God, I now understand that your plan for us — the trust, the faith, the capability given to us — is limitless.

Your faith in us is hidden by our own doubts. In faith, in challenging that faith and finding faith in ourselves, lies an understanding of what humans can do as a species. We need to think much bigger. Where we are going. What we are capable of. What we want to do in this life on this planet. Certainly, I am going to be believing in something bigger for myself.

God, you are much more than I can comprehend. Especially now that I can appreciate the level of complexity I can comprehend, built into this thing called life, it frightens me, wows me, inspires me to know that I may be at only the *first* level of comprehension, level 1.

This cements my faith. We are not an accident. We, us, the Earth. At worst, we are a statistical outcome of a model omni-verse with life-forming ingredients added. But with the souls we possess, the connection we feel, the minds we possess, we are certainly more.

Dear God, keep your faith in me. Help me forge faith in myself by stoking the belief into something bigger and surrendering to the responsibility that comes with it.

Faith

Trust yourself

Dear God,

I believe in something bigger than what I can imagine, what I can fully comprehend. I have gotten to this place by challenging my faith along the way. My beliefs have been forged in the fires of self-doubt, fear of the unknown, fear of personal responsibility, and the weight of the trust and faith the universe has placed in me, in all of us.

My life is up to me, yet my decisions and my actions have a wide impact on others, and those that I make in this life extend beyond what I will be able to see or appreciate. God, the energy I can create is powerful. I trust in myself to do anything I dream, yet have come to appreciate that your faith in me is greater than my faith in myself. Even when I fail, you see it as winning. Losing, winning, learning, growing. Where one stops, another begins.

Somehow, as I begin understanding the scale of life itself, what role we play, the enormity, the vastness — yet even the smallest pieces interconnected — my faith increases, and a calmness is there. I know that, no matter the path and how challenging the journey, the destinations, the outcomes are positive.

God, my trust in myself grows through your faith in me and through my understanding of my potential, my destiny. The limitlessness of the universe and, by default, the limitlessness in me can be frightening and inspiring. I know you'll catch me when I fall, and no matter what, even a failure is progress.

Self-doubt goes away, and with faith in you, we find faith in ourselves. The great irony of life is this: while we have faith in you, your faith in us is greater, and the harder we pray, the more you hold up a mirror. You don't micromanage but have faith in us.

Through prayer, we can find the faith you have in us and the strength to do what we need to do, the courage to stand, and the faith in ourselves. Imagine the confidence of knowing that all outcomes are good. And if all outcomes are good, does that not change planning altogether and our whole approach to life?

Dear God, I'm excited to discover that your faith in me is all the strength I need, but I'm terrified by the responsibility I must accept in my own life, my own outcomes. Help me find the strength to do what I must.

Faith

Faith
Faith in your love
Faith from above
Faith in your plans
Faith in your guiding hand
Faith

Things I can see
Things I can touch
What I cannot see
What I cannot touch
I feel it in my soul
It's the way you touch my heart
Faith

Fear
Fear in myself
For I've failed myself many times before
Why?
Why am I here?
So now it all comes down to me

What you ask of me
What I must do
Fear in my heart
Courage, where are you?
Will you hold my hand?
Will you guide me through?
Faith

Even though it's hard to see
I believe it will be all right
Now it's all up to me
With you here by my side
Faith

Hope

Struggle between good and evil

Dear God,

Why do you allow evil to exist? How can you let the suffering and pain caused by evil to impact the lives of so many people who follow you, your ideas, your teachings?

I have seen the soul of an evil man, one with a black heart and a mask upon his face, hiding in plain sight, working, hunting in the shadows. Like a virus infecting each victim, destroying lives and souls, again and again. I have known and been close to evil, and it's harmed people close to me. I've seen its costume, its charade and games, its depravity.

Evil exists. I've seen it, yet I know that its worst forms are beyond what we can imagine or rationalize.

My hope and prayer is never to fear a dark soul's look, never to look the other way. To have the courage to face it, rid it from its place, and protect and care for those in danger.

Is it because we must understand the balance in life, the value of seeing evil and knowing the full range of behaviors that man is capable of? The depth and the depravity to which we can sink? The line where we cross the spectrum of humanity is a dark place.

God, do we need evil to exist to keep us focused on what is right and what is wrong, the value of good, the need to fight evil, and the drive to make humanity better and better?

In the struggle between good and evil, good always wins. I cannot think of an example where evil triumphs. It flourishes, yes. It's there in ourselves, in mankind, but somehow it fails to win. When we see it, we must attack it. Kill it. And we do. It's in our nature to protect each other and what is right.

Evil is real, and good never eliminates it, since they are different sides of the same coin.

For every time evil rises, good and its purity of purpose rise up against it, buoyed by the hope of mankind and the knowledge of your presence, the knowledge that life can go on, no matter the losses or setbacks. Even in our darkest personal hours — with our own struggle with the good and evil inside us — our hearts and our minds need hope, hope that you will hear our prayers, God, and heal our pain and confusion. Hope that our friends and family will hear our calls. Knowing that no matter the demons, our fears or thoughts, what is on the horizon will be good, peace, and harmony. Good always triumphs over evil.

Dear God, even with the evil I have seen, somehow I know and believe and trust that, in the end, good rises out of the ashes like a shining light in the darkest hours. No matter how dark a man's heart, your love, your expectations, your challenge is this beautiful struggle called life. Evil is overcome by good, and when conquered in its efforts to destroy, comes new life.

Hope

In your mind

Dear God,

In the depth of the night, the darkness sometimes haunts me, and in this darkness, it's only me and my thoughts. The battle between good and evil rages in my mind, despair constantly taking advantage of my worst moments, hope seemingly always outmatched. But somehow, in the morning, when the dawn breaks, with the promise of a new day, a fresh today, hope blooms again. A bright, colorful flower where despair once ruined the soil of my mind.

How do we keep and nurture hope? Where can we draw strength, a purpose, and confidence? How do we keep hope alive and shining in these moments when our minds slip into the darkness?

Not just a lighthouse warning ships of the dangers but a beacon of hope, of love and strength, shining a light on our mind's darkest corner, stamping out the place where evil takes hold, good always conquers, always comes to the rescue.

Armed with this certainty, we can conquer the battles that are raging in our own minds and be ever hopeful. When we wake up, we are flooded with the things we will face in the day ahead and beyond, and before we sleep, we terrorize ourselves replaying the things we should have done but didn't—and the things we wish we'd done differently. Doubt, uncertainty, hopelessness can rage in our minds.

Isn't the struggle over evil, in all its shapes and forms, first won in our minds?

If the battle begins in our own minds, then we must find the strength to establish hope and never let it fade. Transferring the belief in ourselves, empowering our mind that we always, always, have hope for the best possible outcome. Hope in our hearts. Hope in our minds.

Controlling what thoughts we have, we can program ourselves about what to allow in. With the help of the power of positive thinking, "I will, I can, I must," the body follows the mind. But if this is so simple, why do I struggle with keeping negative thoughts out of my mind? Things that will never happen, worrying about loved ones, about money, job, and life?

With a hopeful mind, I know, a hopeful heart is possible. In the mind is where hope begins and where possibilities become endless. The mind must be convinced to truly engage the heart, because the heart might lead a fight, but without the mind believing in it, the fight is lost.

Dear God, please help me master my own mind, own my thoughts of fear, doubt, and despair. In the evenings, plant hope in my mind. Harvest hope in my heart each morning. And feed my mind with thoughts of hope all through the day.

Hope

In your heart

Dear God,

With confidence that good can and will prevail, the fight turns to my heart, unleashing the power of my mind when it's positive and full of belief. My heart yearns for the hope that the mind can control and deliver to direct the heart's emotion, free it from its fear and dread.

A hopeful mind without a hopeful heart is one with no commitment, no purpose, no emotion or drive. Hope clarifies our purpose and cements our commitment. And with the mind and heart aligned, the body and soul follow.

What's the difference—and the connection—between a hopeful heart and hopeful mind? The battle that takes place in my mind—hope versus despair, guilt, fear and hate—once won, can unleash such a powerful effect on my heart. I know the chemicals the brain can control, release. Its physical impact on the heart is powerful.

This hopeful heart pumps blood that's filled with endorphins through the system, positive and electric. Invincible as some warrior, a purveyor of truth, energy armed with hope and acceptance, compassion and love. This hopeful heart is fearless.

Once the mind convinces the heart to enter the battle, there is no turning back. A hopeful heart has the will to never quit, no matter the circumstances, even if the mind has been convinced the struggle can no longer be won.

God, what is it to be hopeful in my life? Is it to remove the feelings of dread when I fear or worry about something that might happen or has happened? Worrying only leaves me feeling ill and doubtful, tired and restless. And yet, I still let the negative thoughts in.

It's positive energy—the aura of hope from within myself—that heals me and protects me. My spirit brings peace and comfort, love and courage to face the day, face life, feel confident.

Hope in our minds enables a hope within, a spiritual hope. A heart full of hope is a powerful heart, one that drives its soul, the human spirit, toward its goals. From the heart comes courage, the will to never quit against the worst circumstances. The mind can convince us that good will triumph, but it's the heart and soul together that fight to victory.

Dear God, help me bring hope into my heart and nurture it, challenge it, use the conviction of purpose in my life. I know if I am filled with hope, then everything I do will be lighter and more purposeful. A hopeful heart is powerful. Hope means that no matter the road, the challenges, or the setbacks, with even a sliver of hope, the heart—and, with it, the body—will endure.

Hope

Hope is contagious

Dear God,

I know what it's like to be around negative people, people with seemingly little or no hope. Their negative energy is palpable and can permeate a room, infect it, draining the life until it's sapped, dead and lifeless. It brings us to the edge of humanity. Hopelessness, despair cling to its host while suffocating him with hate and anger. It's a virus that spreads easily.

But hope. Can you see hope, feel it, recognize it?

A hopeful person's can-do, will-do, always-win attitude is the opposite of the repelling and destructive energy of a negative person. A hopeful person can light up a room. Magnetic, charismatic, positive, energy re-creating, multiplying.

This is one reason I prefer to be around positive people. Hope begets hope, and it unites the mind, heart, and body, broadcasting on a level that accepts, heals, strengthens, drawing in open hearts.

Hope strengthens our resolve. It never rests. It steels us against unimaginable odds and inspires those who see and are transfixed on our efforts. Hope spreads easily, and humans thrive on it.

Hope releases endorphins into our bodies, triggering emotional and physical responses, turning them into energy and a purpose-driven heart, where energy can be felt, shared, and multiplied. Wherever this heart goes, it lights up a room and gives courage to others. Hope begets hope. And a hopeful heart is contagious.

Hope spreads from the mind and heart to the body and soul—then, with that spirit alive, it spreads to others and lifts their hearts and minds. A bond is formed among hopeful souls. A hopeful soul sees the positive in the current and future state, infusing the heart with emotion, conviction, passion and uses its own logic to see what must be done and how best to do it. Every time this hope replaces evil, good people move forward in life.

Dear God, fill my heart with hope and let it, through me, warm the cold souls and strengthen others. Let my hope overflow. Let me generate it, share it, project it.

Prayer

Forget self

Dear God,

In all the years when I saw you in the school's church, in the moments during the service when we were asked to pray, I was never comfortable praying for myself. It somehow felt like asking Santa for presents. I kind of assumed you knew what I needed and when I needed it most. Then a child, I would run through the list of people I could remember and ask you to watch over them, even finishing off with the dog. It felt right to pray for others.

Of course, there are times we want and need to talk to you and ask you for guidance and strength and to listen to our problems. We should try to forget self in prayer, but if we need to pray to God for ourselves, we should also be finding others to help pray for us, with us.

Focusing prayers internally, with their healing vibrations and energies, makes it difficult to imagine working in the same way—except *outwardly*, creating these powerful thoughts and energies and directing them out to find their destinations.

Isn't the positive power of prayer amplified when focused externally? Limitless in scope and effectiveness?

The power of prayer is real, and there are so many examples in life when it has remarkable effects that we can't understand—the strength of its vibration, the depth and the width of its frequency, how long it sustains—especially when many people focus their prayers together.

God, I see how prayers are sent to you from all faiths, the structure, repeating phrases, choruses, rhythms, where every fiber in our being is buzzing in alignment as the prayers echo across the house of faith. The vibrations and frequencies are healing and can be felt far beyond what we understand.

Praying for others is the most powerful expression of acceptance, compassion, and love—recognizing another's needs before our own, dedicating time to pray for them. To forget self and focus on others can lift our spirits, give us energy, peace, and gratitude, as if we were praying for ourselves.

When we focus our compassion on someone else, our own challenges in life seem smaller and less important, and by praying for others, in some way, our prayers are answered.

Dear God, help me to forget my own needs and to focus on others. Praying for another balances my outlook on life, and I know, in your own way, you will answer all my prayers and at the right time.

Prayer

Clear your mind

Dear God,

My earliest memories of praying were as a very young school kid, when the nuns would gather us in church and teach us how to kneel down, fold our hands, close our eyes, and talk to you. We laughed and giggled, nervous at the idea of speaking with an all-seeing and all-knowing God, while trying to imagine what you look like.

The nuns would shush us, and we would quiet down slowly. Eventually the quiet and the vastness of the church, with the nuns' persistent attention on us, would clear our minds. The noise of us children faded in that great space, and we could begin to sit still, slow our breathing, stare in awe at the building, ponder the great men who'd made it under your watchful eye. There, in a house of faith, is where I first felt a sense of peace, calm, acceptance.

Only then the nuns would guide us through short prayers, our minds and bodies at peace, aligned, open. Clear.

Learning that skill from the sisters was something hard to appreciate at the time—the skill of being patient with ourselves, of settling into something and allowing our minds to open up to the peace around us. Even at this very young age, I was taught how to calm down and feel the comfort of relaxing my mind and heart as one.

When I was older and serving as an altar boy, I would be the first person in the church, at 5:45 a.m. I can recall those cold, dark winter mornings, and I felt like they were a magical moment for touching you. There was no one there except me and you. The density of the air, the spirit in the room, the depth of silence. It was always special.

The atmosphere cleared my mind and brought me back to the earlier days with the nuns. I learned how to do it, and, when I'm in the right place, the calmness still comes over me easily. Clearing my mind, opening up thoughts and prayers, nothing in my mind except the clarity of powerful thoughts, prayers, and positive messages about how I can help others and who needs that help. It feels perfect to talk to you. Calm, quiet — my mind can focus on what's important.

Since my childhood days learning from the nuns, I get a sense of awe in other moments and places, and it always reminds me of you. Those are the moments when the silence makes the space larger than when the same space is full of life. Clearing our minds allows us to remove the noise around what to pray for, what's important in the end, what matters the most. It allows our prayers, and what we need, to crystallize in our mind.

Dear God, help me find those places in my life where I can find peace of mind and the calm that comes with it — where I can clear my mind and open up to you. And help me open up my prayers, free from the things that cloud my mind and stop me from aligning with the positive vibrations that are in prayer.

Prayer

Seek the truth, all the truth

Dear God,

Isn't all prayer really a prayer for the truth? If we have truth, we can manage everything else; we understand the way and have the courage to face what's ahead. Seeking truth in prayer seems perfect. It brings clarity to me. I clear my mind, and, at peace, I begin to pray, seeking the truth and with it the strength to accept all that lies ahead.

All of us know the truths in our lives. Our strengths, our weaknesses, and what keeps us awake at night. Our lies, our cheats. Disappointments. Regrets. But God, seeking the truth in prayer is also about facing the truth, the truths I know, the ones I don't ask you about. The ones with which I am ashamed to face you.

Because of this, prayer can be a Pandora's Box. We never know what lies ahead when we seek your help. The road to prayers answered can be winding, beautiful, terrifying, full of both joy and sadness. We have to accept that all truths along the way are part of the prayer, part of the answer. What matters is what we do with the truth that comes, that knowledge.

The truth in prayers is like an onion. Each layer peeled away reveals a deeper truth, a deeper understanding. And the truth at the center of answered prayers can be a real revelation to us.

But often along the way to the real answer, when we think we've found a solution, the answer to our prayers is really only one tool and the first layer. And it unlocks another tool, another way to answer our prayers, and another layer of the onion.

Each tool, each layer we peel away, feels independent. Each tool is different, too. You set each one there for us to find and use to answer our own truths in life. You lead us to find these sets of tools for a reason. They are building blocks in the answers to our prayers. Our job is to find them and use them. You never give an answer to our prayer in the way we can imagine but in a way that teaches us, if we are listening.

Dear God, in my prayers, give me the strength and courage to

face the truth — what I need to know to face the challenges in life. In this moment of closeness with you, I am open and asking for guidance. You have given me the gift of prayer to enable me to be brave, to face the truth, and to display the confidence that you have in me. Armed with my faith that's forged in challenge, I know that I can be a better person. I can overcome the places where I am weak, share my strength with others, and lead when I am needed.

Prayer

Open your heart

Dear God,

How do we know you are listening when we pray? Who hears our prayers? Where do they go—these sounds of thanks, praise, cries of pain, screams of joy and positive thoughts for another? Yet we continue to pray, as we do get answers. They may not come postmarked or with an expiration date, like winning lottery tickets. They may nor result in every ill person being healed.

We find the truth, the courage to use prayer as a way to shape our life.

My mother prayed often. Over the years, she changed how she prayed; I saw it happen. In her younger days, she prayed to, well, *to pray*. It was a *habit*, a way to get through the difficult times in her life, find some peace. Other times, it seemed she almost felt *obligated* to pray.

As she got older, though, she seemed to pray as if she were already communicating with someone, praying across a bridge. She had intent now, a purpose. It was interactive.

She had learned to open her heart in prayer. It took her time to learn how, but her routine of prayer evolved into something else. Her devotion impressed me, made me jealous in a way. She was past faith now, and, God, it was as if she were somehow being held by you when she prayed and no longer feared death. Life, death. They were the same. And she was content that she had done all she was sent to do.

The key for her, I feel, was opening her heart, willing to face the truths of prayer, and really forgetting herself. She prayed outward, constantly for others. She knew all her children well, our strengths, our weaknesses. She prayed for her dead brother, her mother and father, her husband, her daughter. She prayed with the vulnerability of nothing left to lose and nothing to live or die for. At peace, content with life.

Listening to you, God, with this clarity, this openness, truth, this focus and sense of others can bring us to a level of contentment and peace where our heart sings and our mind laughs. As we embrace the vulnerability and joy that comes with the realization that anything is possible—through opening our hearts and accepting—that is a defining moment and the only way we can listen to you.

Prayer is our time to listen to you.

In prayer, we are thinking outside ourselves, forgetting self. We clear our mind and seek the truth, really listen, and open our hearts. We will hear your trust in us, God, your belief that we can do more, are capable of much more. If we can accept the responsibility that is there, for the taking, then anything is possible in life.

We all have the ability to do whatever we desire, whatever we imagine in this life, on this Earth. Faith in you is faith in ourselves, a trust that we will do what we need to do to fulfill our potential, our purpose.

Dear God, be patient as I learn to pray with an open heart and accept the truths that come from prayer. Answer my prayers

through the faith you embody in me, through the trust of sharing the truth that I need to do better for myself and for those around me.

The Prayer

Dear lord
On my knees
Hear my prayers
Begging you please

Sitting here waiting
Believe you're listening
My darkest hours
Having my doubts

Questioning everything
Opening my eyes
Clearing my mind
It's who I am

Open my heart
Seeking truth
Going to find my way
Got no doubts

Seeking justice
In all this prayer
Tell you the truth
It's the courage I need

Dear Lord
On my knees
Guess you've heard my prayers
As I'm begging you, please

Dear Lord
On my feet
Got this covered
Got the courage I need
Dear Lord

www.ingramcontent.com/pod-product-compliance
Ingram Content Group UK Ltd.
Pitfield, Milton Keynes, MK11 3LW, UK
UKHW042018290726
14061UKWH00001BB/66